NO BODY

D1528138

What articulations between bodies, genders and desires are required socio-culturally for recognition of what is human? What happens with those people who do not meet the heteronormative criteria of intelligible life? Are psychology and medicine part of the solution, or part of the problem?

This pioneering book presents a novel analysis of transgender constructions within a clinical setting, examining the experiences of "transsexuality in treatment" interpreted through psychological, feminist, post-structuralist and queer theories. Based on research that includes interviews with the clinic's professionals and users, notes from its group therapy sessions, and analysis of its manuals and scientific productions, the author shows how the psychological sciences not only "treat" transsexuality, but construct it in each of its elements: corporality, sexuality, identity, performances and vulnerability. Looking at the work of philosophers such as Michel Foucault, Judith Butler and Paul B. Preciado, this book also highlights how the productive character of language and other subjectifying technologies are linked to the symbolic and material violence that falls on these bodies, deconstructing the bio-scientific and sociocultural conceptions that nourish the understanding of trans life experiences that are medicalised and psychopathologised.

No Body is a valuable book for students, researchers and professionals in critical psychology, psychiatry and social sciences, and anyone interested in the fields of transsexuality and homo/transphobia, feminism and queer theory, discourse analysis and the construction and signification of the body, gender and sexualities.

Miguel Roselló-Peñaloza is Professor in the School of Psychology at the Universidad Academia de Humanismo Cristiano, Chile. His research interests include feminisms and queer theory; the construction of difference and stigmatisation based on sex, gender and sexual practices; and deconstruction of psychopathology and power relations in science, clinical practices and public politics.

Concepts for Critical Psychology: Disciplinary Boundaries Re-thought

Series editor: Ian Parker

Developments inside psychology that question the history of the discipline and the way it functions in society have led many psychologists to look outside the discipline for new ideas. This series draws on cutting edge critiques from just outside psychology in order to complement and question critical arguments emerging inside. The authors provide new perspectives on subjectivity from disciplinary debates and cultural phenomena adjacent to traditional studies of the individual.

The books in the series are useful for advanced level undergraduate and postgraduate students, researchers and lecturers in psychology and other related disciplines such as cultural studies, geography, literary theory, philosophy, psychotherapy, social work and sociology.

Most recently Published Titles:

Developing Minds
Psychology, neoliberalism and power
Elise Klein

Marxism and Psychoanalysis
In or against Psychology?
David Pavón-Cuéllar

No Body
Clinical Constructions of Gender and Transsexuality –
Pathologisation, Violence and Deconstruction
Miguel Roselló-Peñaloza

NO BODY

Clinical Constructions of
Gender and Transsexuality –
Pathologisation, Violence and
Deconstruction

Miguel Roselló-Peñaloza

Routledge
Taylor & Francis Group

LONDON AND NEW YORK

First published 2018
by Routledge
2 Park Square, Milton Park, Abingdon, Oxon OX14 4RN

and by Routledge
711 Third Avenue, New York, NY 10017

Routledge is an imprint of the Taylor & Francis Group, an informa business

© 2018 Miguel Roselló-Peñaloza

The right of Miguel Roselló-Peñaloza to be identified as author of this work has been asserted by him in accordance with sections 77 and 78 of the Copyright, Designs and Patents Act 1988.

British Library Cataloguing-in-Publication Data
A catalogue record for this book is available from the British Library

Library of Congress Cataloging-in-Publication Data
A catalog record has been requested for this book

ISBN: 978-1-138-22724-8 (hbk)
ISBN: 978-1-138-22725-5 (pbk)
ISBN: 978-1-315-39638-5 (ebk)

Typeset in Bembo
by Apex CoVantage, LLC

To Elena and Miguel

CONTENTS

FOREWORD

One of the popular oft-quoted phrases about gender from Freud which is relayed to students of psychiatry and psychology is "anatomy is destiny". This phrase is endlessly re-circulated to damn psychoanalysis and, in a more brutal twist of the knife, to reinforce exactly the way that most medical psychiatrists and mainstream psychologists already think about the relationship between sexual identity and the body. Psychoanalysis a century ago along with a host of contemporary queer social constructionist approaches to subjectivity are thereby sidelined, and the changing cultural contexts and personal experiences of what it is to be of a certain sex are thereby obscured. This book brings those contexts and experiences out into the open to show how fiercely pitted is "trans" in its many forms against biological body fundamentalists across the psy professions.

The term "anatomy" can now be retrieved from history, along with the voices you will hear in the following pages, to mean, not that the particular frame of the body as defined by the doctor or midwife just after the moment of birth must determine every track of the life-course of the individual, as if the original anatomical structure of the genitals spells out the destiny of the self that is hidden inside the body. Instead, to mean that a particular culturally and historically specific way of conceptually dis-articulating little bits of the body, the significant bits, those accorded significance – the "cutting up" of the body that the word anatomy once described – is given the power to destine the subject to be a "man" or a "woman". Psychiatric practice around the question of gender is saturated with psychological theory, both professionally codified psychological theory and commonsensical notions about the self and gender and biological sex. Each domain of knowledge is organised ideologically to make it seem as if the form of our body speaks directly of an interior fixed "masculinity" or "femininity". *No Body: Clinical Constructions of Gender and Transsexuality – Pathologisation, Violence and Deconstruction* disturbs everyday common sense and medical expertise, enabling contrasting perspectives – from those at the sharp end of psychiatric practice – to be made visible.

This book is about symbolic and actual violence perpetrated by the medical and psy professions against those human subjects viewed as simply locked onto the kinds of bodies that were once described for them, but not recognised as such, as human subjects. It is also about the manifold forms of resistance that are elaborated in speech and action, in interviews and operations that provide the bones of this book. Now these "trans" subjects, with and without the new queer perspectives that inform this book, turn again around their "destined" place as gendered subjects, deconstruct, re-define who they want to be. Psychiatry treats this question of the body as a merely instrumental one, but these subjects redefine how they will be recognised in the clinic. They are of their bodies, Miguel Roselló-Peñaloza shows, having had to live "inside" their bodies as psychological beings of a particular assigned gender. But then, in a practical deconstruction of gender categories that are still routinely imposed on little boys and girls, they speak for themselves, to become, in the process, in social symbolic space "outwith" their bodies, forging a new destiny for themselves in radically different anatomy, if one still imposed by the heterosexual matrix which cuts us into shape.

Ian Parker
University of Manchester

PREFACE

This book brings together results and theoretical reflections arising from research carried out inside a Spanish clinic specialising in the treatment of transsexual people, including the phases of diagnosis, psychotherapeutic accompaniment, endocrinological follow-up, and body modification surgeries. Readers, then, are invited to immerse themselves in the clinic's daily practices and discourses and to probe the chains of statements and clinical demands to which people identified as transsexual are subject when seeking health care. This is an invitation not to analyse transsexuality, but to make the discipline the object of our analysis, to focus our reflections on the biomedical operations that regulate bodies and lives subjectivated in terms of the nosological category.

While we listen to the clinic's mental health professionals' narratives, attend classes taught in a medical school, review its manuals and scientific productions, and listen as well to what trans people who use its services allow us to hear, we will be part of a reflexive process in which theory acquires meaning in social discourses. This is a response to common criticisms that theory (especially in its more constructionist and queer version) is disconnected from realities, a set of abstractions that have little or nothing to say about people's concrete lives. Much to the contrary, we will see how this knowledge permeates and signifies experiences of the regulation of gender and sex in people's concrete and most material lives, from the parcelling of the body, its relation to sexual practices, to the biologisation of identities and their psychopathologisations.

The interest of this immersion course in historically and geographically situated hospital dynamics lies in its institutional discursive source, in that it forms part of the policies of recognition of trans life experiences, and that by connecting to a broader chain of enunciations it participates in the construction and constriction of the lives and subjectivities it conceptualises. As social practices in a dialectic relationship with the institutional, it refers us to internationally delimited prescriptive discourses, framed fundamentally by the Harry Benjamin International Gender Dysphoria Association (HBIGDA), now known as the World Professional Association for Transgender Health (WPATH), and the American Psychological Association (APA).

The principal aim of this work is to contribute to de-psychopathologising gender and sexualities. For this reason, the book gives centre stage to the subjectifying effects of psychological disciplines – in particular, to the most dramatic of them: unintelligibility, which I relate in this book to the symbolic and material death of the bodies involved. Thus, guided by the intention to make explicit what remains hidden behind words, what I propose in these pages is to problematise the logics and basic and universalistic assumptions of science and its reasoning; to dismantle the ideological foundations and effects of violence that lie behind the clinical-social uses of language, by challenging the institutionalised objectivity that legitimise the psychological disciplines' practices and discourses around transsexuality.

This is a work built from my own subjectivity and, therefore, I do not claim that its criticism can be generalised or even that it is necessarily shared. But although this book may fail to disarticulate dominant discourses or to rearticulate their effects on bodies and subjectivities, I hope that at least it will contribute to strengthening practices and discourses that resist pathologisation and other transphobic violence. The practices and discourses of people, social movements and civil rights organisations that in different parts of the world and over many years struggle, in a race against time, to make every life just that: legitimately, life.

ACKNOWLEDGEMENTS

It gives me great pleasure to name and acknowledge the people who, whether they know it or not, have significantly contributed to this book. In the first place, I would like to express my gratitude for her support, inspiration and affectionate guidance during my PhD research, to Teresa Cabruja Ubach, who changed my way of thinking and made possible, in large part, the lines of argument contained in this book, which is hers also. I would also like to thank Erica Burman and Ian Parker for their warm welcome during my life in Manchester, for their thoughts on some of the texts analysed and their confidence in this project.

I would also like to express my gratitude to those interlocutors with whom I discussed some of my thinking, and whose comments and challenges, even disagreements, also inform these lines: Nicole Schmal, Pamela Vaccari, Natalia Rodriguez, Monica Uribe (DIGECIC), China Mills, Mónica Peña, Hannah Berry, Sonia Soans, Jemma Tosh (Discourse Unit), Miquel Missé, Gerard Coll-Planas, Krisna Tolentino and Patricia Castillo. Also to some of the book's first reviewers for their valuable comments: Verena Stolcke, Concepción Fernández and Jan de Vos, whom I also thank for encouraging me to publish this work. To Claudio Cepeda, for his sensitive design for the cover image. And to Sebastian Brett, for his professionalism in translating these words.

I'm also grateful to the institutions that, in one way or another, made this book possible. To the Universitat de Girona for its support given for the realisation of the doctoral thesis that led to this manuscript. To StopSida, especially Adriana Morales, for making the organisation's facilities available for some of the research activities. To the Universidad Academia de Humanismo Cristiano in Santiago, Chile, in particular to the director of the School of Psychology, Francisco Jeanneret, who supported me in finalising this book. To the Universidad Diego Portales and its students, with whom I enthusiastically discussed some of the ideas of this work. To the Spanish hospital where I conducted the research and its professionals, for their invaluable collaboration. And to the National Commission for Scientific and Technological Research (CONICYT) of the Government of Chile, for having financed this study.

I also want to express my gratitude to those who, with their affection and patience, have accompanied me on this writing journey. To my friends, specially to Mery, Carlos, Jeremy, Jose, Angel, Dani, Ricard, Anne, Karina, Andrea, Tomás, Paulina and Viviana. To my family, Elena, Cotty, Miguel and Rodri, for their unshakeable love and confidence, and to Rodrigo, for walking beside me even in the distance.

And, above all, I want to express my deepest gratitude to each of the people who participated in this research and shared with me their experiences of life, their feelings and points of view. Thank you for your trust and generosity, without which this book would have never been written.

INTRODUCTION

Words do not go with the wind. They remain, acquire material force when they are confused with the flesh, with life, when they define it, when they demarcate and obstruct it. Words matter. They construct realities, have effects on concrete worlds and human beings because what we consider real – always contingent, historical and contextual – is determined by our social practices and they are inseparable from language and words. Of course, what we consider to be real has or can have an existence independent of the language in use, but what we know as such is inevitably determined and transformed by what we can say and do with our worlds. Affirming this does not imply, then, denying reality and saying that everything is a matter of language and discourse: it would be naïve not to recognise that we are constrained by material aspects of existence. But it is also beyond doubt that our worlds and lives acquire *other realities* through speech and discourse.

To give an example, the rigid classifications of subjects with respect to their sexual practices and objects of desire have been articulated in terms of diverse specialised nomenclatures, from which we can distinguish ascriptions of identity and a limited specification of individuals. From Benedict Morel's degenerate (1857) via Karl Ulrichs's uranist (1860), the homosexual of Karl Maria Benkert (1869) and Richard von Krafft-Ebing (1886), the inverted of Havelock Ellis (1897) until the Gay is Good of Franklin Kameny in the late 1960s, words have become part of bodies in defining pleasures and ways of life, even particular physiologies and biologies. The subjects that are marked by each of these words, no doubt, are not the same; the effects of these words, the communities they bring together and their political demands, are not either.

The art of medicine has consisted, precisely, in its unlimited descriptive capacity, as well as in its translation of the visible into a specialised nomenclature (Foucault, 1963/2003). This central operation of the discipline in its psychiatric branch is evidenced and acquires legitimacy in the ever more extensive *Diagnostic and Statistical Manual of Mental Disorders* (DSM), the main international catalogue for the objects of the psy sciences, mental illness. Originating in 1952, it is in its third version, published in 1980, that we see Transsexuality catalogued for the first time – 6 years after it was decided, in the only referendum of the manual's history, to exclude homosexuality. This nomenclature would soon be replaced in 1994 in the fourth edition of the manual, which uses the term Gender Identity Disorder, an expression that locates mental pathology in the subjects' gender ascription, that is, by considering certain ascriptions or identifications as healthy and others as unhealthy. The fifth edition of the same manual, launched in 2013 after having proposed the term Gender Incongruence – which assumes a health criterion based on a specific correspondence between gender and sexual recognition of the subject – recovered a term in circulation for several years: Gender Dysphoria. With this term, it was hoped to respond to criticism of the psychopathologisation of trans life experiences, but instead it relocates distress as a matter of gender and of its non-normative ascription, depoliticising transphobia's consequences. Each of these nosologies, then, and with their particular lexical choices, emphasises different elements or normative assessments of the category it defines, altering the requirements for its recognition and, with them, its effects of subjectification.

The physical attacks some bodies are subjected to for reasons of sex, sexual practices, gender ascription and a long etcetera, are often preceded by verbal abuse hurled at people as a mark and a conviction, whose sentence can involve making the body's very material existence disappear. The association between insult and death is transparent. Through words, the body is made vulnerable, recognised as undesirable, and in the very act reduced to an existence that is unfinished or imperfect compared to what is considered life, or legitimate life. The word that is made into an insult not only defines its object, but configures it. It empties the subject of his humanity and reduces him to a body, to flesh that is vulnerable to abuse, rape, beating, deportation, murder.

The verbal aggressions that rain on these bodies are no secret and are undoubtedly known to all. Cassandra, a young Spanish transsexual woman sentenced in March 2017 for publishing comments classified as "glorifying terrorism", has been publicly insulted not for the matter of the sentence, but for her gender ascription: "a poor nutter", "that thing with a moustache", "pervert", and "aberration" are some of the terms used by parliamentarians, television commentators and cybernauts. The bus belonging to the Spanish

Catholic organisation HazteOír (Make Yourself Heard) that toured Spanish streets from early 2017 with the slogan "Boys have a penis. Girls have a vulva. Don't be deceived" is another example of how social powers transit and gain efficacy in language. Words that resonate at the same moment in which social networks are propagating a home video recording the torture of Dandora de Santos (Fortaleza, Brazil), a transsexual woman who was finally murdered after the brutal beating spread on the Internet. One more among so many disappearances, mostly unpunished and silenced. When the disappearance of these bodies is consummated, the prolific world of words seems to vanish.

If language is linked closely to social power, the words that the psy sciences use certainly matter. Every diagnostic process involves a scene in which the subject puts into discourse statements about himself that will then be subject to redefinitions by the authorised professional. What psychiatry and psychology – the top modern authorities in the regulation of populations – name as within their field of expertise structures and transmits what the proper or healthy ways of being a person are and, by extension, also the unhealthy or undesirable ways, where their greatest effects of violence can be traced.

To say that the clinic – and specifically the psychiatric and psychological clinic – exerts violence on the lives with which it works is nothing new. However, it is still a troubling statement. Of course, saying this is not to deny the good intentions that legitimise every practice involved in clinical work, whose operations are articulated in the use of language. That would be senseless and imply denying its often beneficial effects. But it would also be senseless not to recognise the dangers its narratives hold when they are presented as universal theories of the subject. More so when these reproduce exclusionary social conventions and norms transmuted into canons of health and good mental health; when they constrain human experience and introject in the subject different types of social violence directed against their bodies.

The recognition policies involved in the work of psy disciplines converge in naming and providing intelligibility to social distress and the intimate experiences associated with it. But what is intelligible, what we can read and inscribe in a framework of understanding, is limited to its possibility of being textualised, to certain limited fields of registration. To put it differently, the alternatives for the recognition of human experience are given in advance by the discourses at our disposal and how they are administered. As such, they constitute the field in which power relations are exercised, full of obstructions, subordinations, normalisations and silencings – and also of psychopathologisations, when psychiatric nosology deforms and introjects in people their social experiences of oppression. Knowledge, then, can well construct non-recognitions when the institutionalised and hegemonic uses of language do not recognise, deny or preclude life experiences that do not correspond to its normative prescriptions. It can even make the experience precarious and the life itself unintelligible (Butler, 2009a).

We know that one cannot live in any fashion, and not because there exists something like an original limit to the imaginable ways of inhabiting the world, but because the discourses configure specific limits for social recognitions, and these limits are what define what is possible, what exists, and the impossible, the unthinkable, or what should not exist. Of course, subjective experiences are not determined univocally by the social meanings transmitted by words – which are always polyphonic and liable to resignifications – but social experiences do appear as delimited by them more or less homogeneously within certain contextual frameworks. Belonging to one or another social category, for example, according to how it is culturally signified and valued, can be reason enough for enjoying more or fewer rights and privileges than other citizens. The various forms of social recognition or non-recognition, along with other cultural and material elements, establish limits for possible life experiences and make certain subjective and political constellations unviable.

This governability of the subject by psychology, as in other modern disciplines (medicine, pedagogy, prevention policies or public hygiene, etc.), does not work by direct oppression or coercion but, rather, through a regulation that is exercised as naturalisation and that pursues normalisation. This is because the discipline does not work like an encyclopaedia that describes and documents realities contained in people, and then develops the most appropriate therapeutic techniques to restore their wellbeing. It operates as technologies of government do: by producing knowledge and, with it, realities; managing subjectivities by means of an authoritarian science-tinged knowledge that indicates the ideal models of being a person. It restricts the spaces for the production of discourses that are not psychologised or medicalised, leaving people with no alternative other than to accept and submit to psychological knowledge (Rose, 1989, 2007; Ibáñez, 1996; Cabruja, 1996, 1998; Parker, 2007).

Psy disciplines are part of the constrictions that produce and reproduce conventions and social norms at the service of power, and that – given the abstract character of their constructions – affect the lives not only of those most harmed by the discourses but everybody's (Burman, 2003). Such is the case, for example, with the various sexual pleasures that diverge from these conventions and social norms, and which end up becoming perversions or paraphilias, concepts against which all sexuality is scrutinised from its most intimate relational or subjective spaces. Or with transsexuality, in which gender norms reveal their virtualism and are unveiled as part of a complex technology with which clothes, body movements and feelings are subject to strict inspection.

1
DECONSTRUCTING THE PSYCHIATRIC BODY

Politics of recognition

In this first chapter, I shall problematise the construction and regulation of bodies, sexual practices and gender ascriptions or identifications by putting narratives, discourses and clinical practices in dialogue with some theoretical contributions that allow us to approach the body, gender and sexualities as constructed categories, as products of history and ideology in which power relations are articulated – relations that we shall explore and unravel throughout this book by bringing the violence they produce to the surface. Of course, body, gender and sexualities are differentiable and in many aspects respond to distinct normative constructions (Butler, 2009b), but here we shall explore them in their interconnections through, for instance, Foucault's device of sexuality (1976/1978), Judith Butler's heterosexual matrix (1990/1999) or the sexopolitical regime of Beatriz (now Paul) Preciado (2003). At the end of our review, no body will remain on which gender and sexualities are inscribed, but sexed bodies that are regulated and moulded by their technical and discursive operations. Nor will there remain a possible gender that is recognisable without coherence in the carnal parts that constitute the idea of the body as a limit and a unit (Butler, 1990/1999; 2004); nor will there be an intelligible sexuality without the social meanings that shape corporality as technological productions of gender (De Lauretis, 1987; Preciado, 2000/2011).

With the device of sexuality and its arrangements that are constituent parts of the technologies of power, an entire political theory emerged about the intelligibility of subjects as always-sexed beings. It was announced by Foucault when he said,

> It is through sex – in fact, an imaginary point determined by the deployment of sexuality – that each individual has to pass in order to have access to his own intelligibility [. . .] the whole of his body [. . .] to his identity.
>
> *(Foucault, 1976/1978, pp. 155–156)*

The proposed disarticulation of sex allowed the biological, universalistic and essentialist representations and explanations of peoples' ways of being and feeling to be theoretically surpassed. "Sex" now became an artificial unity and also the cause of every fiction of unity. Now not only were bodies understood to be docile (Foucault, 1975/1995), but pleasures, the very idea of a *oneself* and the social recognition of subjects came to be anchored in a double axis between the disciplining of the body and the regulation of the population. At the very heart of what seemed most intimate and personal we now find the tangle of power relations in their most productive expression.

Technologies of sex that are also of gender, as Teresa de Lauretis points out (1987), where gender transcends any derivation of a non-imaginary sexual difference. Gender as process and "the product of various social technologies, such as cinema, and of institutionalised discourses, epistemologies, and critical practices, as well as practices of daily life" (De Lauretis, 1987, p. 2). Like Foucault's sexuality (1976/1978), but exceeding it in the differential construction of the feminine and masculine as a social relationship, it is the "set of effects produced in bodies, behaviours, and social relations" (p. 127).

Together with this notion of the Technology of Gender, the conceptualisation of heterosexuality as a political regime – as a specific programme for the production of *life* (Wittig, 1992) – would extend our understanding of bio-power (or regulation of the population with the purpose of maximising life) to the production of heterosexual male and female bodies[1] (Preciado, 2000/2011, 2003, 2005, 2008/2015). Expressed differently, the new understanding of heterosexuality as an economic and reproductive regime denaturalises the classification of human bodies into men and women. Henceforth, it would no longer be possible to think of sex as prior to gender, or as a sign on which the latter is written: on the contrary, sex indistinguishable from gender, a category that is "fully politically invested, naturalized but not natural" (Butler, 1990/1999, p. 143).

With Judith Butler, who questions the apparently pre-discursive nature of the body in Foucault's analyses – as pliant matter on which history and norm are written – gender came to be the analytical centre of desires, bodies and sexual practices. As a discursive practice structured around heterosexuality, gender became the gravitational centre for the production of *human* persons. Access to social recognition, to subjection, will depend on its normative adjustment and productive efficiency. The lack of this recognition, on the contrary, would constitute the precariousness of lives that cease to count as *lives* (Butler, 1990/1999, 2009a, 2009b).

By re-articulating Judith Butler's theory of performativity (1990/1999, 1993a, 1997), in which gender emerges as a regulated (and sanctioned) product of ritualistic acts with naturalising effects, the counter-sexuality of Paul Preciado (2000/2011) takes us toward the disarticulation of heterocentrism by means of a "deconstruction of the organ-origin" (p. 70). Preciado multiplies Monique Wittig's division of the sexed body by borrowing the cyborg politics of Donna Haraway (1991) and turns the body into a prosthetic construction confused with the technologies of artifice.

This re-articulation combines with some of the criticisms that gender performativity theory has received, generally reflecting an understanding of the latter as a discursive product that fails to recognise the body's materiality and vulnerability, in line with the conflictive interpretation of social constructionism as a negation of reality (Parker, 1992; Ibáñez, 1996). For example, Preciado (2000/2011) points out that Butler had "placed in parentheses both the materiality of the practices of imitation as well as the effects of inscription on the body that accompany every performance" (p. 80), failing to recognise the convergence of different axes of oppression and the carnal consequences of performative violence. In a similar vein, Cristina Molina (2003) questions Butler for looking sideways at the question of the social organisations of power, and specifically "their dimension as an expression of patriarchal power" (p. 126), which can turn the counter-practices of gender into a suicidal proposal for those who do not hold positions of power. I mention these criticisms and contributions (among a wide range of others) to show that this theorising has not been problem-free, specifically in its relation with transsexuality, a controversy that was quickly aroused by the use of the parody of drag as an example. Butler, however, addresses many of these criticisms in the explanations she gives in her text *Critically Queer* (1993b), where she points out that the regulation of gender is hierarchical and coercive and that this produces concrete and material effects on bodies and their disciplining through, for example, criminalisations and psychopathologisations mediated by gender norms.

In this chapter, we will follow these conceptual movements, although not in linear fashion. Of the chapter's two sections, the first, which I call

"Unrecognisable bodies, impossible sexualities", attempts to retrace the path followed by the control and regulation of bodies, sexualities and identities. My intention is to provide a scheme that serves to show how bodies – specifically of persons referred to as transsexual – are disciplined through a complex network in which sex, desire and gender become indistinguishable. In the second section, "Clinical violence and juridical lack of recognition: the production of no-bodies", the analysis ranges through three dimensions that coerce and produce the gender (un)intelligibility of transsexual persons: diagnostic demands, the articulation between medicine and jurisprudence, and the construction of otherness.

Section 1. Unrecognisable bodies, impossible sexualities

It is difficult, if not impossible, to resolve the question of whether an anatomical body exists prior to any operation of perception (Butler, 1990/1999), because the body as we perceive it is the only body we know and with which we relate. To attempt it is to enter a machinery of fictions in which nature re-emerges as a criterion of truth while the materiality of flesh is disfigured and reconstructed in the linguistic act of apprehending it. What we can resolve is where we locate the reality, not of flesh, but of flesh as we know it, for we must accept that it is quite impossible – because it is unthinkable – to conceive of flesh without accepting the constraints of language in which flesh only becomes thinkable as constitutive of a body.

This is why I repeatedly choose the notion of flesh rather than body when I want to stress the partialisation of the body and the different potentialities of these parts to signify the body as a whole. In doing so, I appropriate Butler's criticism about the supposed prediscursiveness of the body in Foucauldian theory, as a disciplining of or on the body (Foucault, 1976/1978). I also agree with what Thomas Laqueur (1990/2003) seems to suggest when he states that the philosopher "longs for a nonconstructed utopian space in the flesh from which to undermine 'bio-power'" (pp. 13–14). As a body, flesh acquires cohesion and material limits that make possible the rhetoric of inside/out (Fuss, 1991); its partialisation, as a counterpart, carries with it the possibility of dis-articulation and resignification. In other words, the body is not unitary but fragmented, and only fragmented it becomes unitary (Butler, 1990/1999). As a unit, it is discursively constructed by a multiplicity of partialities that gain sense in relation to others and that, taken together, make possible a complete and unified body. Thus, a piece of flesh without any reference to the organ it comes from or the animal species it belongs to – without a complete set of references that make it comprehensible as "flesh of" – is unthinkable. Flesh would cease to be flesh and become unidentifiable matter. A body, on the other hand, can still be a body even if it does not have the totality of its parts; an incomplete body, if you like, compared to a fictitious whole – but a body nonetheless.

The human body is disarticulated, transformed, signified and in short, constructed by social technologies like language, but also by a limitless number of material technologies that cohabit with the flesh and make it possible as a body and a sexed body. These include electronic devices, surgical interventions, cosmetics, transport, organ enhancement, pills, cinema and pornography, latex shields, food industry and the whole long etcetera that not only give the body its place and function but produce it and merge with it to the point of indistinguishability. On some occasions, they intervene solely at the level of the parts, reconstructing them or potentiating their isolation; on others they centralise the body as a whole on the part, making the part into its foundation. Two phallocentred examples: the condom, as the *body*'s "contamination" barrier against HIV through the isolation of the poli-penetrative homosexual penis, associated with death by constructing AIDS as a venereal disease (Bersani, 2010); and vasodilators, as erection optimiser and, therewith, producer of the masculinity that the penis and its copulative function signify (Preciado, 2008/2015).

Sexuality, a productive cross between knowledge and power, configures the body, precisely, by discriminating between its parts, dividing it as a whole, disuniting it in its demand for sexual unity. As Butler puts it, "that penis, vagina, breasts and so forth, are named sexual parts is both a restriction of the erogenous body to those parts and a fragmentation of the body as a whole" (Butler, 1990/1999, p. 146). It is this division and specialisation of certain parts that makes it possible to represent the body as a single sexed image. To be understood as either male or female, then, the body finds itself restricted to those parts that are signified as being sexual, and it is from them that it emerges in its dichotomous specificity as a whole being, since "only one body per gendered subject is 'right'. All other bodies are wrong" (Stone, 1991, p. 297).

Sorry, but you (don't) have it

If with Preciado (2000/2011) we understand sexual technology as "a kind of abstract 'operating table' on which certain corporal zones are trimmed as organs" (p. 116), and that since the 1950s – with the entry of post-industrial capitalism, of aesthetic-reproductive technologies, and of gender identity in the intersex clinic – the sex/gender system has ceased to rest on the division of sexual and reproductive work and has stabilised on the penis as a sexual signifier, we can see how the *trimming* of the penis becomes the key sign of the difference between the sexes – a sign capable of creating men or masculine identities (and deny feminine ones) even in the presence of other non-sexual or *less* sexual body parts, as we will see in the following fragment, which begins our journey round the gender clinic and what its various actors tell us:

> It annoys me when a woman who doesn't want to be operated tells me that she is a woman. No, no way, because you have a penis and a penis doesn't belong to a woman.
>
> *(Isabel,[2] MtF, interview)*

What this fragment tells us is that the presence of a penis in a feminine or feminised body has the potential to invalidate a recognition of the body as a *woman* by its hyper-signifying presence. The presence of a penis, and its being noted, seems to be enough to reduce corporality as a whole to that specific portion of it (Maffia & Cabral, 2003; Nieto, 2008) and goes further in signifying the body as not-female due to its phallic component. Once the penis is noted, all the other attributes seem secondary: "*a woman* who doesn't want to be operated" disappears behind a genital that does not allow her recognition as such. Somehow, behind the coherence of the parts there seem to be first and second order sexual organs in sexually signifying the body, so that the presence of one is enough to overcome the significance of another in the way the body is textualised.

The woman appears to be there, but only as a phantasm of a woman, refutable because the presence of a penis denies her status. The desire not to eliminate this body part that is capable of gendering an entire body imposes a verdict on what would be necessary to constitute a woman, which in the last analysis would imply the penis as an absence. Without it mattering that it was once there, what counts is (the desire that) it be there no longer, and that it not invalidate the body as a whole by its presence. A body that is in-valid by being unrecognisable by the coherence of its parts according to the regulatory heterosexual matrix, or "that grid of cultural intelligibility through which bodies, genders, and desires are naturalized" (Butler, 1990/1999, p. 194), which demands a single relationship between body parts and the recognition of gender or sexual membership. Any maladjustment, incoherence or lack of recognition will make the body unviable, an error or a pathology.

Access to a viable body, then, requires not only the presence of sexual parts but that these be consistent with one another and the whole. Incoherence or *incongruence*[3] leads to unintelligibility and unintelligibility to a body that is unplaceable. Neither women with a penis, nor men with a vagina or even breasts, enter recognisable territory: the medicalisation of gynecomastia is proof of that. Various body strategies, like those involved in dressing, can potentially conceal from public inspection the presence of an anatomical trait capable of denying or confirming recognition by creating a mirage of intelligibility. This was exactly the strategy responsible for the polemic surrounding the film *The Crying Game* by director Neil Jordan (1992). In the film, the invisibility of the penis and the superb feminine performance of actor Jaye Davidson makes Dil, the protagonist, unquestionably female for viewers until the moment comes when she removes her clothes, and the camera closes on the unexpected penis, creating one of cinema's great best-kept-secret scenes. A close-up that in the film, and not uncommonly in sexual encounters of transsexual people, unleashes the violence with which the disciplining of the body acts to regulate gender.

Gender is straight

> Only and exclusively, that orifice that can receive an adult penis is defined as a vagina.
>
> (Preciado, 2000/2011, p. 125)

An encounter between two naked bodies, then, is what creates one of the scenes of maximum tension for recognition, and by means of it, intelligibility. In order to introduce this dimension, we shall review what traditionally happens with sex and gender assignation to babies recognised to be intersexual.

The infant's body, operationalised as a declarative object, is defined as that of a boy or a girl on the basis, exclusively, of its morphology and genital aesthetic; what is visible and how it is represented is the logic on which sexual difference is constructed. With this primacy of the visual, no other corporal or behavioural element appears to be distinguishable for assigning sex. The individual's chromosomic composition will not determine their assignment to a sex, mainly due to the time required to obtain the result and the socio-legal urgency of declaring a sex (Maffía & Cabral, 2003). Nor will the presence or absence of certain sexual gonads, at least not since the last century, when medical technology developed sufficiently to be able to work on what was anatomically visible, naturalising sexual dualism and making invisible the anatomical variations observable in so-called intersexual babies (Dreger, 1998).

When the newborn baby's anatomy presents ambiguities to the clinical-cultural eye able to make − or rather, configure − the distinction, the assignation will be based on the baby's future genital capacity to maintain heterosexual sexual relations. This assessment is based on a visual discrimination by the expert medical eye that, based on criteria of shape and size, *constructs* rather than identifies heterosexual organs (Preciado, 2000/2011). Thus, together with the interpellation of gender or performative invocation, the body itself is produced according to prescriptive objectives regarding its − future and imagined − sexual practices. Let us look at this in more detail.

When the body of an intersex baby is born − enters the clinical scene − a sexual determination protocol is set in motion, in which a presupposed sexual activity will define the baby's surgical future (Kitzinger, 1999). By way of example, according to what Fausto-Sterling calls the "size rule" (2000, p. 59) and Preciado "centimetre politics" (2000/2011, p. 129), an infant's clitoris greater than 0.9 centimetres but less than 2.5 centimetres, which biomedical science establishes as the minimum average length for a penis, is at risk of amputation or reduction. A similar surgical destiny awaits a penis shorter than a range from 2.5 to 1.5 centimetres (Kessler, 1998/2002; Fisher, 2003), an arbitrary criterion that makes it *too* small to suppose a future capacity for heterosexual copulation. The baby then will be assigned to be a girl, together with the surgical construction of a vagina (if there is none) deep enough to supposedly allow future penetration. This is why the heterosexual marriage of adults whose genitals were surgically intervened in infancy is often taken as a measure of the success of the decision and clinical practice in the case of intersex babies (Kitzinger, 1999). Similarly, the success of vaginaplastia in transsexual persons is measured normally by the neovagina's subsequent capacity for heterosexual coital practices (Hausman, 1992; Stone, 1991).

There is, therefore, interdependence between sexing the body and the body's sexual activity, in that the anatomy gains sexual intelligibility through its supposed capacity for heterosexual copulation (Rich, 1980/2003; Wittig, 1992). Not just capacity, but desire is involved too (although surgical interventions, with their often harmful effects on the newborn's body, do not take this into consideration and even obstruct it). This is because a relation is presupposed between the organ to be corrected and its use or orientation toward genitals configured as *opposite*. In other words, it is the presupposition (and prescription) of a heterosexual erotic desire that in the last analysis will determine the assignation of a sexual category to the body in question. It is true that the surgeons and medical team involved in this alteration of the healthy body of the newborn will not discuss the future sexual practices of the infant whose body has been victimised by their operations, but the very conception (and technological construction) of a male or female body by virtue of its genitals' capacity for sexual interaction and copulation stages a concrete sexual practice centred on the genital encounter. To put it differently, just-born bodies are visualised as if they were having sex.

What I am saying is that a (supposed and future) desire for a body sexually categorised as opposite in terms of its genitality – based on a logic of the copulative potential of organs – is constituted as a determinant of the sexual assignation of the body in question. In other words, the configuration of sexual desire on the basis of the assumption of genital complementarity in sexual relations and the production of pleasure – or heterosexuality as an imperative in sexual assignation that substitutes for gonads as indicators of reproductive potential (Hausman, 1992) – turns into a key construct for the identification and adjustment of bodies as belonging exclusively to the realm of masculinity or femininity.

To have it is not enough: it must work (but not anywhere)

With this recognition of bodies as coherently sexed only when oriented to a specific genital sexual practice in mind, I suggest a reading of the following fragment, with which we continue our exploration of the discourses of the gender clinic, this time through the comments of one of its mental health professionals:

> For example, there are female transsexuals who work as prostitutes, and what makes them go on earning money is having a penis and having a penis that works. But when these women have to penetrate a man, ok, they do it for money, they often have to take Viagra or other things, you know, to be able to function, but they don't get aroused doing that or enjoy it, like it goes against their attitude, against their sexual role, know what I mean? So it's almost a contradiction to find a female transsexual who enjoys doing that, such a male sexual role, know what I mean? So there's a sort of contradiction there, there's something that says, "Hey! Wait a moment, evaluate that".
>
> *(Psychologist, interview)*

What is presented here as "almost a contradiction" is the coexistence of a given gender, the feminine, with the *enjoyment* of a sexual activity which, although directed toward men and therefore within the heterosexual norm of mutual copulative desire, is performed by using a penis which should not be there. "Women [who] have to penetrate a man" implies that the woman is present, constructed discursively despite the presence of the penis, but of a penis that is inert, unserviceable, a mistaken carnal addition that is incapable of channelling any sexual desire that goes "against their attitude, against their sexual role". When the penis "works", that is, when is capable of penetrating and the person finds satisfaction in this sexual dynamic, it comes into contradiction with the recognition of the subject–woman and suspends the gender recognition that the person declares in the clinic, questioning the diagnosis of gender dysphoria (an indispensable requirement for access to the medical protocols for body modifications). Gender, then, appears to be drawn in relation to a concrete sexual attitude, deviation from which is only conceivable through the example of prostitution, the need to earn money, and the use of a chemical erection enhancer (which only works, moreover, when there is a sexual stimulus that generates enough sexual pleasure to produce an erection).

As we saw with the intersex clinic, the recognisable body, the heterosexual body, is the product of a specific functional arrangement of its organ components. A *natural* penis qualifies as such by its capacity to penetrate a vagina or another potentially penetrable orifice, while a vagina is defined by its potential to be penetrated by a penis. This is why Paul Preciado interprets and appropriates the famous (but never spoken) phrase "I have no vagina" of Monique Wittig, debtor of the equally famous dictum "lesbians are not women" (Wittig, 1992, p. 32). Preciado points out that "a vagina that does not allow itself to be territorialised by hetero intercourse is unnatural, deficient and even 'unhealthy like a lung that has never breathed'" (Preciado, 2005, p. 128). In reverse, a penis is a penis, with a potential to involve the whole body with its masculinising effect, only as long as it penetrates. A penis that does not become erect, that does not penetrate, is not, in a strict sense, the penis of a *man*, and for this reason, according to heterocentric thinking's functional division of the flesh, does not affect the assignment *woman*. Instead, the penis comes to represent a feature with no more meaning than that of a useless appendage and, for that reason, is surgically removable, as in fact happens in the transsexual clinic. This is the logic that prevents a woman from being a woman when she penetrates a man, more so if she takes pleasure in it. She cannot be a woman if she has a *real* penis. The act is not only illegitimate but also illegible: returning to the words of the fragment, it is "almost a contradiction". In these terms, a transsexual woman will always and above all be a man, in that the feminised body becomes the accessory of a penis that is not the useless accessory of the trans body that the clinic prescribes.

If we understand by heteronormativity the political-cultural privilege of heterosexuality as the axis of intimacy and the pillar supporting social organisation and participation (Berlant & Warner, 1998), perhaps we can find here one of the most problematic aspects of the heteronormative management and recognition of the body and sexuality. In this partialisation and functional anchorage of the eroticised and sexualised organ – with its potential of signifying the body as a whole as a member of one or other of the opposed sexual pairs – a transsexual woman who copulates with and penetrates a man and gets pleasure and potentially an orgasm engages in a non-heterosexual activity which can be read as a repetition and imitation of heterosexual coitus, although in fact it is disarticulated. The reason, among others, is that the body she copulates with is not the one to which she is constrained by the genital-centred heterosexual regime. Returning to Monique Wittig's non-phrase, "I have no vagina" – insofar as this is defined by its heterosexual territorialisation – and if we change it (not to her liking, I fear) to "I have no penis", partialisation and functionality are shown to be precarious signs for the recognition of gender, now questioned by the sex of the object of desire. If "lesbians are not women", the body-with-penis who practises coitus with another body-with-penis is not a man either because the penetrative potential of the penis diverts to a non-heterosexual orifice. It even may not play a penetrative role in the coital relation, even when it preserves and shows its erectile potential and continues to be an active part of the erotic practice. For this reason, a perfectly territorialised penis, functional and potentially penetrative, will not be sufficient to genderise the subject when the sexual encounter involves another body-with-penis, even though it actually penetrates. We cannot state calmly that it is the penis of a man, or even more complicated, that it is actually a penis. There is no space in which to define these practices, for example, as heterosexual coitus with the possibility that a woman penetrates a man with her *natural* penis. This is why for this specific heteronormative configuration of the flesh and its sexual assignment, a transsexual woman with a functional penis penetrating a body-with-penis and taking pleasure in it, lacks all sexual intelligibility.

Impossible sexual practices?

> Older adolescents, when sexually active, usually do not show or allow partners to touch their sexual organs. For adults with an aversion towards their genitals, sexual activity is constrained by the preference that their genitals not be seen or touched by their partners.
>
> (APA, 2013, p. 454)

From the obstacles imposed by the heterosexual economy of discourses on the fluidity of desire, one can comprehend the difficulties experienced by some transsexual persons over sexual practices, a sphere that has become a whole field of study for medicine devoted to genital modification surgery (see, e.g., De Cuypere et al., 2005; Wierckx et al., 2011). Already in 1956, the psychoanalyst Jean-Marc Alby was stating, in a discourse characteristic of the discipline and its psychologising effects, that the sexuality of (feminine) transsexual persons was the object of severe repression, including abstinence from sexual practices in advance of genital surgery because of the denial of the feminine image their erections might generate, and with a libido characterised by elements of narcissism, fetishism, exhibitionism and masochism (Mercader, 1994/1997) – a whole field of pathologies and dissatisfaction.

Indeed, in the latest version of the *Diagnostic and Statistical Manual of Mental Disorders*, DSM-5 (APA, 2013), one can trace this construction of the *impossible* sexuality of persons defined by this category. The quote at the start of this section shows how, as I have been arguing, the political technologies of sex call into question the sexuality of transsexual persons, by their apportionment of the body and hyper-signification of the so-called sex organs. These body portions must not be *shown, seen* or *touched*, since the mise-en-scène of pleasures through this special reduction of the body calls into question the very intelligibility of their bodies. The presence, functionality and obtainment of pleasure, and indeed the partner's desire for those body portions have the potential of denying the ever-precarious reach of the ideals of coherence that gender categories demand.

However, the genitalisation and apportionment of gender, and with it of sexuality, does not always imply a negation of sexual life or of using the sexualised parts of the body. Although it is a Discourse with capital letters, bodies are never mapped by it entirely. There are chances of movement, of freedom within the constricted spaces implied in the normative demands for the recognition of intelligible bodies and sexualities. Thus, for example, use of the vagina as a support for a dildo reveals the prosthetic and plastic character of the sexes (Preciado, 2000/2011), changing the heterosexual significance of the body and of the genitals according to their functional possibilities. The pleasurable coital use of the penis in transsexual women is by no means uncommon, above all when there is a displacement of sexual practice and the orientation of sexual desire as coherent constructs with the transsexualising process – in what the literature has called transhomosexuality or homosexual sexual orientation according to the destined gender – even when the practice may not involve an appropriation and the desirability of their own genitality. On occasions, indeed, the body's unintelligibility may be only limited to the gaze and the logic of the visible (Kessler, 1998), outside of which it is articulated in specific strategies of incorporation of the sexual – as we can see in the following fragment, in which a rupture is established with the heteronormative use of the breasts in an erotic contact, displaced from their centrality but incorporated within the sexual territory:

> It had to be with the lights off and the way of touching had to be totally different [. . .] From the waist up she had to . . . her hands had to go from the neck to the belly, never from the belly to the neck.
>
> *(Andreu, FtM, interview)*

These and many other disarticulations of the heteronormative scripts for the place of the body and its portions in erotic life show us the arbitrariness of the meanings and functions prescribed for the sexed body, and reveal the violent effects of the social technologies for its control, prescription and erotic construction. The body continues to be the only one perceivable, but its same violent subdivision entails properties that disarticulate the limits of the body as such, making it malleable and plastic by the force of the same discursive oppression. If "the regulation of 'sex' finds no sex there, external to its own regulation" (Butler, 1992, p. 349), this regulation not only limits as it constructs but also includes and configures the possibilities entailed by its own individual and collective management. What I have addressed here as the heterosexual constriction and formation of the body and its pleasures, then, in no way determines unequivocally the bodies and sexualities it articulates. They depend on it, they form part of it, but it should not be forgotten that at the same time they have the potential to denaturalise its borders.

Section 2. Clinical violence and juridical lack of recognition: the production of no-bodies

A common worry in talking about non-hegemonic gender and sexual identities is over the appropriateness of using the categories of gender normative ascription – or even of gender short and simple, if we consider that gender is always normative – in order to define the identities or socio-political locations of the subjectivities in question. Joshua Gamson (1995), for example, ponders over the viability and political-strategic usefulness of using ethnic/ essentialist identities – sometimes necessary for collective resistance and political demands[4] – as against the dissolution of identity categories as bases of oppression and social control, and thus an obstacle to resistance. Didier Eribon asks himself a similar question when he says, "it is necessary to criticise this submission to the normative categories which are precisely those of subjugation" (2000, p. 81), and so does Paul Preciado when he tells us about the "normalising and disciplinary effects of any identity formation" (2005, p. 165).

But to disarticulate these schemes, to rebel against the *gender hell*, as Riki Anne Wilchins (1997) invites us to do, can turn into a threat against oneself when obtaining health guarantees is involved or the social recognition needed to exercise citizenship, and indeed to live with less vulnerability. This is because *gender terrorism*, in Kate Bornstein's terms (1994), does not lie in non-normative gender and sexual identities, but in an inner relationship – in the very construct of gender and its different forms of violence. Violence that is used to harass others about the consequences of crossing the limits of gender and that not infrequently also takes the shape of demands of transgression, directed at transsexual or transsexualised bodies accused of being not progressive enough in their search for corporalities and recognition of unequivocal gender (Namaste, 2005). As Henry Rubin (2003) states, "transsexuals per se are neither *essentially* gender normative nor *essentially* gender subversive. Judging transsexuals as a group by their commitment to the gender revolution obscures [their] heterogeneity" (p. 164).

The political circumstances and balance of forces that make it necessary to cite the normative discourse of compulsory binomial gender ascription refer to the urgency of the legitimation and legibility of one's own body when it is constructed as abject. If we understand by abject "that which has been expelled from the body, discharged as excrement, literally rendered 'Other'" (Butler, 1990/1999, p. 169), we are talking about corporalities that have been expelled, evacuated or excreted from inside the normative boundaries. Consequently, exteriority is reduced to an impossible contrivance, because not only does it come from the internal but also *is* the internal – it constitutes it as identity and difference. Because of this, Monique Wittig is wrong when she speaks of lesbianism as "a position outside the system of oppression that the sexes produce" (Preciado, 2005, p. 118), and also Foucault, who appears to contradict himself when analysing the life of the hermaphrodite Herculine Barbin by talking of "the happy limbo of a non-identity" (Foucault, 1980, p. xiii). On the contrary, there is no sexuality, nor are there bodies or desires outside the norm. Thinking that there are is to collaborate with a power hidden behind the phony smile of libertarian condescendence.

If we continue with this line of argument, we can state that if there is a transgression in transsexuality, it does not lie in the invocation of – and here I borrow from Butler's analysis of Wittig and de Beauvoir's *becoming a woman*:

> the figure of the androgyne nor some hypothetical "third gender", nor is it a transcendence of the binary. Instead, it is an internal subversion

in which the binary is both presupposed and proliferated to the point where it no longer makes sense.

(Butler, 1990/1999, p. 162)

Transsexuality, then, as a fiction of externality within the frames that configure the bimorphism of bodies and for this reason, the citation of the normative discourse implies an opening of these frames, of their limits; an extension toward the surroundings that the discourse denies. While the invocation of binomial gender does not escape from the objective of optimising life as *specific forms of life*, it reverts the fiction of externality to the internal, falsehood into truth. Imitating the duality of genders, it restores to that duality an image of totality that disarticulates it by not offering it an exterior in which to be contained.

Following Didier Eribon's reading of Foucauldian resistance (Eribon, 1999/2004), "reverse discourse or counterdiscourse is thus not necessarily another discourse, an opposite discourse. It might be the same discourse, relying on the same categories, but turning them around or transforming their meaning" (p. 313). And as the same author asserts in a different text, "those who most want to integrate into society are those most likely to disrupt the established order" (Eribon, 2000, p. 35), precisely by their capacity to disarticulate and disable normative notions by including what has been defined as alien and opposite.

Of course, with the foregoing I do not claim to have solved the question with which we began this section. Having recourse to the categories of man and woman and taking them to be the sign and nucleus of an identity also contributes to strengthening the power relations that force these bodies to search for intelligibility, to reconfigure their exteriority, with violent normalising consequences for their lives. Whether the norm is destabilised or reinforced in its plasticity is an even more complicated question to answer. It is probably not enough to make identity categories into problematic constructions by bringing to them a multiple concurrence of sexual discourses (Butler, 1990/1999). If the purpose is to disarticulate their oppressive consequences, the "labour of symbolic destruction and construction aimed at imposing new categories of perception and appreciation" (Bourdieu, 1998/2001, p. 123) cannot be abandoned.

The diagnostic requirement of submission

The construct of gender, its own executioner, and the gender clinic, its main gatekeeper, exhort the body to accept its normative submission by configuring it as a mistake. The rhetoric of the wrong body, which defines the transsexual person's *sickness* and *treatment*, works because it ignores or fails to recognise that the body's material existence is only apprehensible in terms of the discourses and practices that constitute it and enable its existence as a body, rather than an unrecognisable jumble of carnal parts. To say that the body is wrong, then, is a contradiction in terms. Of course, the body suffers, gets sick and dies, and that has nothing to do with language, but it is also true that this *reality* acquires another reality through language (Parker, 1992; Ibáñez, 1996). Unveiling[5] the *mistake*, the process that provides the basis for a diagnosis of gender dysphoria is no more than the effect of psychiatry as a producer of subjects in deficit, a fantasy that nevertheless demands the surrender of the person who submits to its imaginative machinery, and that will be later transformed into a legally unchallengeable scientific certificate. Paradoxically, the gender clinic will demand the invocation and performance of a gender that, on the contrary, *is never wrong*, and is present forever and since forever, in which any shortfall of confirmation risks suspension of the possibility of being read within the limits of intelligibility.

Being ascribed the category of *man*, for example, means entering a circuit of coherences and spatial and temporal units that constrain bodies, sexualities and affects so that they conform to the limits of intelligibility in which *a man* becomes possible. The following fragment from an interview with a transsexual man in treatment shows how the clinical diagnosis works by exhorting the subject to undergo an ideal adjustment within these limits, backed by an implicit threat of suspending the diagnosis or denying recognition:

> My former partner came with me and she later made her come in as well, on her own, and I waited for her outside. She asked her how her sexual relations with me were, if I let myself be touched, if . . . etc. She also asked me since when, more or less, I knew about it, she asked me things that were of . . . for her, analysable, right? "And as for you, when was the last time you put on a dress, the last time you . . . ?" You know? Something characteristic of a girl, a feminine girl, or a girl.
>
> *(Rodrigo, FtM, interview)*

This text evinces the criteria that lead to a diagnosis of transsexuality and of masculinity as well. It evokes a scene in which the interview departs from the physician-patient context and enters the social life of the subject under analysis. Not allowing himself to be touched is one of the signs of nonsexuality, interpreted as the product of an incoherence or inconsistency in what is supposed to be the rigid anchorage between sex-gender and desires. When the diagnostic scenario extends to other persons treated as witnesses, not only the subject's body but also their network of relations face demands of coherence, as a guarantor of recognition and also of control of the same unity (Davies & Harré, 1990). It refers to a recognised and recognisable sense of identity, supported by the managed body and social regulation.

The question about the time at which the experience became knowledge refers to a search for a turning point in subjective-corporal experience, but above all for the moment at which the subject gained knowledge about the category of sex and its urgent demands for coherence as a condition of intelligibility. In other words, the question is directed toward the entry of the subjectivation with which the device of sexuality operates, toward the moment at which the subject recognised his own unrecognisability, "as if a page of a book suddenly became conscious and felt itself *being read aloud* without being able *to read itself*" (Sartre, 1952/1963, p. 41).

The gendered construction of body parts ventures beyond the body and extends to accessories, in this case the "dress". This shows us once more, as the example of the dildo did, the prosthetic character of bodies, where each part that is interpreted as belonging to the subject – such as breasts or penis – is *also* nothing but a prosthesis loaded with meanings (Preciado, 2008/2015). Use of the "dress" becomes an analysable sign that contains the truth about the subject's gender, a part-and-whole that exceeds – by hiding or being the only strategy of body modification available – the portions of the body that do not correspond with the normative gender ideal.

In general, what we see is that the diagnostic scene is based on ideals of coherence that require that each of the parts that comprise the sexed body coincide, including those that are not strictly carnal; among them social relations, life history, and sexual pleasures. Regulations that, when they detect some incoherence, open the way for the intervention of medical protocols of adjustment or anchorage. One of the first steps in these regulatory (and productive) operations is the requirement of demonstrating that an ascribed gender is not only declaratory but also coherent with the other parts that together construct the fiction of unity required to configure a sexed body. The requirement is to *live* according to the gender with which the person identifies. This requirement, known as the real-life test, is one of the most common clinical conditions for a diagnostic confirmation, even though it has disappeared as a formal requirement in the latest version of Standards of Care (WPATH, 2011).[6] Now let us see how a gender clinic psychiatrist explains this phase or requirement to her students:

> Imagine that one of you comes and tells me that you feel like a boy, okay? [. . .] Then we'd say, fine if you really feel you are a boy, be consistent, prove it, start . . . and if you are going to change your appearance

and later change your . . . start to comment on them, tell about them, to see if you are really capable of going so far.

(Medical class)

The foregoing is, in short, a specific request for proof or demonstration to confirm that the declaration correlates with the reality, which implies to assume, of course, that *feeling* like a man or a woman is something for which there are established verification criteria. It refers us to gender identity as a truth located inside the subject but recognisable in the field of the visible. Gender understood as an expressed truth is the basis of this evaluative operation, which exhorts the body to shed any attributes that allow the recognition of a mistaken gender (the assigned one) and substitute them for those that lay bare the destined gender (the ascribed one). This very possibility of passing from the recognition of one gender to another reflects the plasticity of the acts that characterise the one and the other, revealed in the same operation of not repeating, of deforming or parodically repeating (Butler, 1988). This is possible precisely because "gender attributes are not expressive [. . .] but performative" (Butler, 1990/1999, p. 180), and therefore it is not a question of revealing or demonstrating gender with reference to certain visible and verifiable criteria, but rather that it is these same criteria, acts or attributes that *construct* what in appearance they are displaying. The demand for demonstration, then, is in reality a demand for imitation, for gender production and not of gender expression. It is the disciplinary demand of a series of gender performances that have been discursively disfigured in proof, with the effect of giving gender and the construct of its identification an essential and natural status.

The assigned gender, anchored and revealed in signs that are constructed as unequivocal proof of sexual membership, is considered to be a false origin that must be purged and is only there because of an error in the signs' emergence (that is the rhetoric of the wrong body we referred to earlier). Its correction or abandonment is channelled through declarations and performances in coherence, distorted into tests of the truth that the initial clinical demand for the gender of destination was nothing but the gender of origin that had mistakenly not been assigned, in that "performing it well provides the reassurance that there is an essentialism of gender identity after all" (Butler, 1988, p. 528). As Sandy Stone (1991) points out, referring to the Stanford Gender Dysphoria Program, the dispositive works as a *school of protocol*, meaning a clinic that not only works diagnosing and treating transsexuality, but also producing women and men who are readable through the prescription of unerring gender performances capable of confirming that the gender identity claimed by the subject is *real*.

The construct of gender identity which sustains this exercise – and appears constructed as a truth that is prior to the clinical scene and, as such, demonstrable through a history of habits and appearances – is in fact a sophisticated technology of gender regulation that functions as an amalgam of carnality and its social meanings. Its paradox consists in that, by demanding confirmation of the gender of destination as the gender of origin, it demands also a biographical rupture of the life sequence. This is what the clinical/social demand of living in coherence with the ascribed gender implies, a rite of passage (Billings & Urban, 1982) that if it is not adhered to, or is resisted, can lead to expulsion from the protocols of assistance, and even refusal of the technologies for body modification. This is so even when continuing with the protocol may imply new forms of social violence, as recounted by one of the transsexual women in treatment:

> Me going like that as a girl, people give you a bad look. They insult you and I was going to school and I couldn't go like that, because you have to join in . . . so that they can laugh. No way [. . .] you can't do what they ask you, it's to commit suicide. I'd rather jump off the balcony than do that.
>
> *(Ariel, MtF, interview)*

It is clear that the discourse of sex as unitary and expressive, put into action in this demand of the clinic, is not only attributable to medical science or the *psy sciences* (Rose, 1985; Gordo & Parker, 1999). The different dominant social discourses on gender and the dichotomous sexual descriptions of species have mutated over time to the point of changing into natural, unquestionable cultural truths made indispensable for the social recognition of subjects, infiltrated in society as if on constant guard, like a socialised medical quasi-consciousness (Foucault, 1963/2003). Yet it is also clear that the clinical space continues to be one of the most important devices for actualising, regulating and (re)producing this sexual truth. Through clinic techniques of trans-sexualisation, bodies and their relational experiences are constrained in the most patent way to fit into exclusive and excluding frameworks of sexuation. Long before the scalpel goes into action, diagnostic requirements impose the first constrictions on attaining the *new gender* as a destiny. And in that destiny, in the exigencies of the route to get there, the interdiscursive relation with legal institutions is an unavoidable element in understanding how the articulation of discourses produces, and yet denies, access to the gender intelligibility of subjects.

Juridico-clinical regulations: the double violence of gender

The intersection and interdependence of the legal and medical discourses is one of the major points of tension in the regulation of bodies and the legal recognition of transsexual persons. The category of *sex* knits together the law and the medical regulations in configuring access requirements within the limits of cultural intelligibility.

In Spanish law, until 2007 surgical modification of the genitals was indispensable for a person requesting to register a gender change in official identity documents.[7] Until then, the genitals were the Spanish state's final proof of the requester's *true* gender.[8] With the approval of the Spanish state's law of gender identity – Law 3/2007 of the General Courts, passed on 15 March 2007 – the surgical requirement to register a sex change was dropped and replaced by a diagnosis of gender dysphoria and 2 years of hormone treatment. In appearance, this legal change – which conceives transsexuality to be a diagnosable and treatable pathology (Garaizabal, 2010) – dispenses with the genital organs and therewith the heterosexual uniqueness of the body in recognising the gender alleged by the subject. In appearance, because the specific medicalisation demanded merely implies *another* way of disciplining the body and its parts.

In the case of female transsexual persons, the requirement of hormonation over 2 years involves proof of penile erectile dysfunction – which is one of the effects of hormonal treatment – for the same number of years, and presumably into the future. This guarantees the fiction of non-exercise of a sexuality that is *incoherent* with the gender alleged, by converting the penis into a sexually unserviceable and therefore potentially extractable addition. In the case of male transsexual persons, the medical criterion recommends carrying out a hysterectomy (extraction of the uterus) and oophorectomy (extraction of the ovaries) because of the possible health risks attached to their permanence during hormonal treatment. With this change, one imagines (I say only imagines) that the criterion of hormonation supposes the elimination or atrophy of organs that are heavily gender-charged – the penis, as the centre of sexual activity, and as the origin of sexual difference (Preciado, 2000/2011), the bastion of masculinity; and ovaries and uterus, menstruation being the emblem of femininity (Ussher, 1989), a sign of the maternal-woman, producer of desirable life.

In the intersection of both discourses, there is what we could consider a spatial reconfiguration of what are considered sexual signs, from the sphere of the genitals' presence to that of (reproductive?) functionality. However, that does not imply abandonment of the presence of primary sexed signs as the configurers of sexual differentiation. Despite the apparent relaxation of requirements, the reorganisation of sexual signs forms a new basis for distinguishing bodies that now precedes visible morphology. The clinical-social-legal eye is not blind to the presence of genitalia, but goes a step further by installing gender binomialism in the organs' sexual reason: male penetration and female fertility. It is true that this opens the door to social recognition without need for the scalpel, and even grants legitimacy to bodies without gender-anatomic coherence. Yet, given that discourse constructs and not only describes (Foucault, 1961/2006, 1969/1972; Fairclough, 1989/2001; Parker, 1992, 1996; Burman, 1996; Ibáñez, 1996; Cabruja, Íñiguez & Vázquez, 2000), we cannot ignore that bodies and genders are being constructed here by means of an even more anticipated elimination of intermediary states. Its basis is more brutal because it extends even beyond the genital image – which it does not deny as a sexual sign since the requirement is only invoked when the latter is interpreted as incoherent – to the physiological potential for pleasure (masculine) and reproduction (feminine).

If we consider the preceding at a discursive level, we can see how the particular uses of language in the legal and clinical fields, or discursive genres (Fairclough, 1992/2000), interconnect in a complex political technology that colonises the different orders in which discourses on sexuality operate. What we might call the same discourse of sex as being unique and unitary, true and necessary, is administered by medicine through the technological possibility of analysis and sex-revealing physical change, and by the law as the recognition of signs that make the subject of law differentiable, biographically continuous and socially responsible. Thus, interdependent, they intervene with new effects in power relations centred on gender and sexualities, with the interdiscursive need to recur necessarily to one another to configure them.

One of the most problematic fields in which both discursive genres are articulated is gender violence. Availing myself of the Spanish, in which "gender" and "genre" share the same word (*género*), I propose to understand such violence as being double: on the one hand based on *gender* as a "sophisticated technology that manufactures sexual bodies" (Preciado, 2000/2011, p. 21) that are coherent and hierarchically organised, and on the other as constituted by the discursive *genres* of the medical and juridical fields. Of course, by saying this I am not suggesting that it is a case of different types of violence. I refer always to gender violence as the "result of a logic of creation of othernesses in order to refine the techniques of government, which finds a mechanism for controlling bodies and the lives of populations in the construction of gendered sexual difference" (Bonet, 2007, p. 45). Gender violence, because gender, as a normative category that gives access to the subject as such, is the reason for acts of violence directed to the body (Cabruja, 2007). What I propose is that the intersection of the medical and juridical discursive genres configures and justifies new violent operations on the body in a coercive production of gender. To emphasise the violent effects of this interdiscursive relationship I shall refer to gender violence as double violence of gender when I want to stress this dual institutional voice in the regulation of gender and disciplining of the body.

The articulation of gender recognition leads to a forced adjustment of the flesh following the criteria of the two institutions examined here: medicine and the law, the most significant regulators of the legible life. A double violence of gender is produced that, in the need for adjustment, pushes the body into technological interventions in order to comply with the requirement of intelligibility that both disciplines have jointly instituted. Both genres, in a kind of double colonisation, signify sex as single and unitary, true and necessary, but rearticulate its signs and recognition requirements according to the demands of each institution. To put it differently, it is an exercise similar to that of the International Olympic Committee, which in 1986 withdrew Spanish athlete María Martínez Patiño's licence due to her XY kariotype, only to reinstate it in 1988 after confirming her insensitivity to androgens, thus revealing the arbitrariness or scientific-legal inconsistency in rearticulating the *true sex*, although without suspending or questioning it.

Although the truth of sex does not change, it is displaced and repositioned, showing not only its artificiality but also the violence with which the individual is altered and subjugated in the name of a truth that is no more than a complex encounter between two social practices that participate in the regulation of gender. The surgical requirement mentioned earlier – still necessary in the majority of European countries to have a sex change recorded in official documents – is an example; another is the requirement of sterilisation (TGEU, 2016) that reminds us so graphically of the violence of eugenics legislations belonging, but not exclusively, to Nazi Germany. The flesh subjectified in non-recognition and compelled to gain recognition through access to corporality (necessarily sexed) is an object and product of violence in achieving its inscription within the frames of what is recognisable, precisely at the meeting point of the conditions implied by the category of gender for each institution in the production of a sexed body.

On occasions, it is this intersection of the two discursive genres which justifies, ultimately, trans persons' access to the medical protocols, even when there is no intention either of a clinical recognition per se or a body adjustment in the terms clinical medicine envisages. The need to obtain a document certifying *gender dysphoria*, for example, is indispensable to begin the procedures for legal recognition in the great majority of countries with laws that allow registers to be changed.[9] Here, the violence of medicalisation, one of the forms that gender violence assumes in our society – being a technology that demands submission to achieve gender recognition – is articulated at the intersection of these institutional demands, and is exercised via a pathologising and euphemistic diagnosis, a rhetorical strategy that disguises a series of body control practices as scientific-clinical discovery.

We speak of discourses that constitute relations of violence in their forms, in what they pursue and how they obtain it. It is *violence* because it imposes rigid models of how to be, and does so by denying the conditions of possibility for subjection, for intelligibility, forcing the flesh to be a normative body by means of chemistry and the scalpel. It is *gender* violence because its root is the disciplinary imposition of one sex / one gender for each body; body as a specific configuration of parts, functions and desires.

This is how this violence works, as an amalgam of ideology and technology among whose effects is also to make it impossible (or at least very difficult) to recognise one's body as one's own, desirable and adequate. The fragments that follow are from persons under treatment in the gender clinic. I reproduce them here because they show us precisely the body's annulment as an adequate and coherent unit and how certain parts are felt to be alien or in contradiction with the gender with which the subject identifies:

> I really don't look at myself in the mirror. When I look at myself is when I have a compression T-shirt on [. . .] Without the T-shirt, no, because I find it impossible.
>
> *(Jordi, FtM, interview)*

> At this moment in my life, the only thing I want is to be able to look in the mirror and be a complete man [. . .] Right now it's of no importance to me whether [my penis] works more or works less.
>
> *(Joan, FtM, interview)*

Let there be no doubt: metaphysical considerations apart, managing one's own body is not necessarily an act that harms the body like an aggression, but is part of the very same construction of one's body as an amalgam of sexually signified prostheses. If the meaning of body parts is not only anchored in the discourses of power but is constructed by them, modification of those parts is no more than an exercise coherent with the body's prosthetic character, and therefore adjustable as the technology and one's desires allow. However, we cannot forget that desires are configured in relation to the ideological framework of institutions and their technologies, and for that reason, what is presented as an individual desire is not free of their exercise of violence and disciplining. As Judith Butler (2009b) says,

> If what "I" want is only produced in relation to what is wanted from me, then the idea of "my own" desire turns out to be something of a misnomer [. . .] a desire that is and is not one's own.
>
> *(p. xi)*

If what is ideologically *a body* does not embrace all the possible anatomies and subjectivities, it is precisely because it is shaped in terms of ideals, not originals; it approximates certain models and installs them as *desirable* according to their correspondence with regulatory purposes, while non-correspondence or deviation is configured as *un*desirable.

What is this no-body?

If we assume that "heterosexuality is not simply a question of sexual orientation,[10] or even of sexual practices but a political regime that produces, among other things, the possibility of the body's recognition as an organic unity" (Preciado, 2005, p. 127), whose truths of intelligibility are constituted by a (heterosexual) matrix that constructs artificial links with gender productions and sexualities (Butler, 1990/1999), we can see how the configurations of *deviation* or *error* are not simply a displacement of the *other* bodies toward the outside. First, because, as we have seen, there is no discourse or subject external to power. Second, because it is not only a question of bodies that do not comply with certain norms of intelligibility, but above all of the construction of new bodies from the norm, as a model product (yes, the reverse too) from which interiority acquires intelligibility.

The *disadjustment* of bodies and subjectivities to gender norms makes them unrecognisable and therefore un-nameable, beings "who appear to be persons but who fail to conform to the gendered norms of cultural intelligibility by which persons are defined" (Butler, 1990/1999, p. 23). If personal practices and identities do not reflect the unity, continuity and coherence required by the heterosexual matrix, the *being* will have no access to recognition and its very social construction as a *subject* denied. But if we agree that bodies are not pre-discursive and therefore that the logic that applies to them cannot be one of expulsion, but of excretion (Kristeva, 1982), what bodies and subjectivities are constructed? Who are these beings who only "appear to be persons"? Or, to quote a question explicitly formulated by Judith Butler (2009b), "What do we call those who do not and cannot appear as 'subjects' within hegemonic discourse?" (p. iii). The two quotes that follow from two women undergoing hospital treatment provide a clear and explicit answer:

> And people in the street do the same, please. People are very cruel. And I don't want to appear a monster or anything ridiculous, I don't want them to laugh at me.
>
> *(Ariel, MtF, interview)*

> I was looking so much like a man, that no, I said, "what do I do now?" and I was thinking, "I'm going to become a monster".
>
> *(Isabel, MtF, interview)*

The colloquial use of monstrosity shows us how in the popular imaginary bodies that do not conform to heterosexual demands are signified, as well as the social effects of their recognition. Transsexual bodies appear like a monstrous or impossible space, vulnerable, an object of shame and social rejection because of their incoherently sexed image, and liable to be pointed at by others as a result of their categorisation, which as Pierre Bourdieu (1990) points out derives etymologically from the Greek *katêgorien*, from which stems the English word "category", meaning "accuse publicly" (p. 34). The subject is marked as an object through the insult, which does not necessarily have to happen in reality but is always sufficient because of the certainty that it can happen (Eribon, 2000, 1999/2004).

If "the body only has sense if it is sexed, [then] a body without sex is monstrous" (Preciado, 2000/2011, p. 120). Monstrous, for not being recognisable as either male or female, for not being a human body. As in the case of intersex babies, "the body of unidentified sex [. . .] is considered to be a regression to a 'primitive' and vegetative state, when the sexes have not yet been compartmentalised" (Preciado, 2005, p. 127). Monstrous, then, because of their construction as unrecognisable corporalities, and therefore objects of fright-rejection-insult; unnatural beings, outside the natural order not just by being incoherently sexed but also by involution: dragged toward the *flesh*, deprived of *body*. This is what the colloquial use of the term "monster" used in the fragments means. In English the word alludes to "something extraordinary or unnatural"; "an ugly or deformed person, animal or thing", and/or "a mythical creature which is part animal and part human, or combines elements of two or more animal forms".[11]

It refers us to a dual dimension of the monstrous. In the first place, it takes us to one of its pre-eighteenth-century medico-juridical forms that Foucault (1999/2003) defined, understood as mixtures (of the animal and human kingdoms, of two individuals, of two species, of life and death, of forms and/or sexes); as "the transgression of natural limits, the transgression of classifications, of the table, and of the law as table" (p. 63). And at the same time it refers us to a post-nineteenth-century monstrosity, in which it is no longer a mixture or a "transgression of everything that separates one sex from another [. . .] [but of] eccentricities, kinds of imperfection, errors of nature" (p. 72) that make *true monstrosity* possible, more of behaviour than nature, to which it refers in the last instance.[12]

If for Derrida (2001) monstrosity is what cannot be apprehended in terms of what exists, then either it demands an extension of the limits of the possible or it falls within the territory of the non-existent. If we go back to the semantic study of the term and we look for a specific meaning in medicine, we might venture the answer for these two possible alternatives: a monster is "a fetus, neonate, or individual with a gross congenital malformation, usually of a degree *incompatible with life*".[13] What cannot be apprehended, then, not as an opening or challenge to taxonomies and the logic of the possible, but as something that cannot be read, something made non-existent. At this point, I partially agree with Vivien Namaste (2005) when she states that transsexual persons "are not, in point of fact, produced by medical and psychiatric institutions. Rather, they are continually *erased* from the institutional world [. . .] excluded from its terms of reference" (p. 3). I only agree in part because I prefer to suggest that medical and psychiatric institutions indeed participate in the construction of transsexuality and the persons subjectivated by the category. Although not unequivocally, not without resistances, and not without new openings and meanings, they do participate in their construction precisely by erasing them, based on this non-recognition within the boundaries of the possible. To make of transsexuality something not-possible is one of the most significant effects of the gender clinic, as we shall see at the end of this book. A not-possibility that exists, however; one that is not outside the frames of intelligibility but which the frames themselves constitute through a process of excretory construction, or as Judith Butler says, through Iris Young and Julia Kristeva, "This is the mode by which the Others become shit" (Butler, 1990/1999, p. 170).

With these points in mind, we can read the prescription of *impossible sexuality* that we discussed in the first section, namely that a sexual relation between two bodies that are not bodies is impossible. The denied sexuality of transsexuality, which as we saw does not map bodies entirely and, in fact, is subject to reconfigurations of practices and corporalities, is a consequence of this impossibility of reading bodies and sexual practices that are not textualised. In turning to sexual pleasure, bodies are reappropriated and deformed by heteronormative regulation, recognised as unrecognisable, and therefore silenced or negated. In the words of Didier Eribon (2000), "the great structure of oppression applied specifically to homosexuals [and transsexuals, we may add] is the obligation to be silent and conceal what they are". I understand this obligation to be silent as not only against uttering a discourse that presents a person's own experience politically as legitimate or desirable, for example, but more so the demand to not allow their own experience and corporality to speak. In other words, to make it impossible for the body itself to show its unrecognisability both in the public sphere and in the intimacy of sexual pleasure. Flesh and sexualities that, before hiding from sight, have been silenced by denying them any possibility of becoming text, of being body and subject. A clinical-social production of un-natural beings, of insultable practices, of uninhabitable identities, of bodies that are *no-bodies*.

Notes

1 This despite Monique Wittig's view of heterosexuality as "a structure of domination that explains women's oppression throughout history" (Preciado, 2005, p. 115), and not as an apparatus that produces sexuality.
2 All names have been changed to protect the anonymity of those who contributed to the research.
3 According to the drafts of DSM-5 (available on the APA website between 2010 and 2012), the first name suggested to replace Gender Identity Disorder (APA, 1994) was Gender Incongruence. It was widely questioned by activists and academia because "under its influence, all non-normative gender positions that do not fit perfectly into the traditional gender poles could be medicalised" (Ortega and Romero, 2012, p. 5). Finally, the APA (2013) opted for the name of Gender Dysphoria. However, the term *incongruence* appears repeatedly in descriptions of the category.
4 Without having recourse to essential identities but rather to shared experiences of subordination, Erica Burman (1992) calls attention to the dangers of dissolving into multiple differences the relations of oppression that are common to feminisms. Emphasising the need to break down the universal and homogenising model of the *woman* and to visibilise its exclusions, she notes that

> There is a sense in which we need to affirm for strategic purposes that there is some commonality in the positions and experiences of women by virtue of our subordination. Experiences of oppression, then, not only constrain and

produce our subjectivities (with very material effects); they also permit some basis for unity. (p. 48)

5 I use here the verb *to unveil* as a euphemism for the clinical-surgical construction of the *sexual truth*. In the words of Paul Preciado (2008/2015): "The truth of sex is not unveiling, it is *sex design*" (p. 35).

6 Publication that serves as an international guide for the integral attention of transsexual people. Until its previous version, published in 2001, the real-life test had to be successful for at least three months before moving on to the next phase or hormone treatment.

7 According to the human rights organisation Transgender Europe (TGEU, 2016), 23 European countries still require genital surgery for registry change, including countries such as France, Switzerland and Belgium. The United Kingdom's Gender Recognition Act (2004) has allowed registration change without the requirement of genital surgery since 2005; Argentina's Gender Identity Law 26,743 (2012) was the first in the world to eliminate the diagnosis and all medicalisation from the requirements for legal recognition of ascribed gender.

8 Note that despite certification of surgical modification of the genitalia and achievement of a registry change, Spanish law did not include the possibility of celebrating certain legal acts, such as marriage (Toldrà, 2000).

9 According to the same organisation (TGEU, 2016), the only European countries that did not require diagnostic certification for a registry change in 2016 were Denmark, Ireland, Malta and Norway.

10 As Eve Kosofsky Sedgwick (1990) reminds us, sexual orientation is an arbitrarily made construct that envisages desire as channelled toward bodies dichotomised as male or female, and does not envisage the infinite possible objects of desire.

11 According to the online version of the Oxford English Dictionary, available at www.oed.com.

12 Foucault uses these notions to show how the attribution of monstrosity (associated with hermaphroditism) transitions from a juridico-natural system to a juridico-moral one, or a field of criminal monstrosity. It should be mentioned here that before the entry into modernity, as Felix Vázquez and Andrés Moreno (1997) explain, hermaphroditism was a possibility of nature. It is only since the eighteenth century, with the proscription of any sexual duplicity that there has been a widespread refusal to admit the possibility of hermaphroditism. In the nineteenth century the scientific explanation of monstrosity emerges, which confirms the existence of a single true sex and describes apparent sexual duplicity as a genital malformation. If in the Middle Ages the image of the monster belonged to the satanic order, now that it finds a natural explanation there is nothing to distance it from hermaphroditism.

13 According to the online version of the Oxford English Dictionary, available at www.oed.com.

2

THE BIOLOGISATION OF GENDER

Somatic fictions of identity

In the last chapter, we looked at how the *psy sciences* construct the body – specifically the sexed body – and how their practices and discourses articulate with the social recognitions mediated by the legal frameworks, doing violence to the bodies of transsexual or transsexualised persons with their juridico-clinical demands. At this point, we can advance no further in our analysis of the psychosocial effects of the gender clinic without knowing the *scientific* reasons that bind transsexual persons to medical protocols. For the gender clinic to deal with its domain, stake its claim for expert knowledge and exercise its interventions by right, transsexuality must have an intelligible explanation in the field of what is medically intervenable: the body, its developments and functions.

The stubborn search for explanations of the forms of life, apart from its intentions and volition, is not an innocent activity. As Adrienne Rich points out (1980/2003) about lesbian sexuality,[1] searching for the causes of any phenomenon, whether the approach adopted is essentialist, constructivist or any variation in between, implies the conceptualisation of a difference as needing an explanation. For this reason, it is always a performative reinforcement of normative conceptions, which, being the axis from which to measure *deviation*, are not themselves in need of any explanation at all. By this logic, to trace causes is itself an exercise of exclusion by simple performative repetition disguised as empiricism, theoretical sufficiency or scientific interest. It excludes because it constructs subjects/objects as (still) inexplicable or unintelligible, while the norm (statistical-political, or the political normativisation of what statistics make visible) rests in the security of being the only true one. The other is simply *other*, without existence, or as Diane Fuss (1991) says, "it stands in for, paradoxically, that which stands without" (p. 3).

However, the constitution of the external in opposition to the internal, as we saw in the previous chapter, is little more than a fiction. Little more, because despite its often disastrous consequences, the external, the different, as interiority excreted (Kristeva, 1982) marks the limits and indeed the content of the axis of expulsion, of the normative or inner. Interiority, for this reason, is impossible without this play between *shortfalls from* and *adhesions to* the normal/normative; above all, it is what is contained within the contours traced through expulsion. In Rosi Braidotti's words (2001):

> By virtue of its organic, as well as structural, proximity to the dominant subject-position, the monstrous other helps define "sameness". Normality is, after all – as Canguilhem teaches us – the zero-degree of monstrosity.
>
> *(p. 388)*

In reverse, given this ambiguity of the inside/out, the need to explain *differentness* means resorting to the intelligible as a mechanism to capture what has been exteriorised. In this exercise of the inner as the epistemological source, what the external has of internal is made to emerge: the same logics of normative configuration. The purpose may well be different, but the effect, as a product of this fiction of a border is to give it visibility, to trace its links with the normative even if only in terms of the unrecognisable, like deviation, alteration, maladjustment or any other derivation of what we might call a rhetoric *of the mistake*. In the very production of knowledge, then, borders are made flexible, strict demarcations blurred, and the security of the normal/ normative is made problematic, as well as of what science configures as abject health or life.

Of course, the foregoing does not imply abandoning critical study of explanations of forms of life just because we recognise their inherent instability. Challenging them is necessary not only to construct alternative narratives, and therewith new possibilities of inhabitability, but also because, in this permeability between the internal and the external, between what is inside and what is outside, the danger of the explanatory, of the fictions of *bringing to light* by means of rhetorics of the mistaken or undesirable, is incalculable. In her epistemology of the closet, Eve Kosofsky Sedgwick (1990) suggests the "obsolescence of essentialist/constructivist" dichotomies in the search for the ontogeny of the sexual preferences with which people are characterised, because, among other things, in the same analytical exercise the discussion implies, it is difficult to "divorce these terms [. . .] from the essentially gay-genocidal nexuses of thought" (p. 40).[2] Indeed, looking for the causes of what is constructed as sick or unhealthy often implies, also, the search for its possibilities of *cure*, and consequently of extermination. One of the many examples is the tragic story of the homosexuals in the Nazi extermination camp of Buchenwald, and the experiments of the sadly celebrated medic Carl Vaernet, based on his hypotheses of the endocrinological causes of homo-sexuality, and whose *healing* aims even went so far as to implant the testicles of animals, with lethal consequences.[3] I add here in quotes the comment of the sociologist and trans activist Miquel Missé (2010), "the day they 'discover' the accursed cause of our 'disease' we will cease to talk of transsexual persons, because we will not exist" (p. 274).

The sexed brain

A useful exercise in approaching the clinical-scientific explanations of trans-sexuality is to explore the discursive articulations present in the transmission of knowledge. So I invite you to return to the lecture room, and along with the students of this medical class, listen to how the psychiatrist explains the biological origin of gender ascriptions, whether normative or not:[4]

> And if I am a judge and I say to you, well, you are doctors and you have to tell me really if this person here is a man or a woman, okay? So, we have . . . you have as doctors . . . me, as a judge, it's very important for me to know if it's a man or a woman, because there are important legal repercussions.
>
> *(Medical class)*

In this fragment, we encounter once more the juridico-clinical inter-discursivity we approached earlier. Here, it works as a borderline case exam-ple that actualise the medical function's expertise in determining *true sex*, a capacity and knowledge that officially it has exercised in the courts since the eighteenth century (Vázquez & Moreno, 1997). From this judgment a series of "legal repercussions" will derive, among them the possibility of exercising the right of matrimony and parentage (at least in most countries of the world), as well as the possibility of gender recognition and the resulting changes in official records. Of course, this invitation to the students does not allow them to think outside the interdiscursive boundaries within which the question is put: the field constituted by medicine and jurisprudence, an articulation of argument that functions as a discursive obstruction (Fairclough, 1992/2000), by enclosing the field of what is sayable and thinkable.

To answer this question, the class continues by setting out the different possibilities available for the assignment of sex according to scientific knowledge: chromosomes, internal genitals, external genitals and secondary sex characteristics. However, none of them will be decisive in establishing the subject's gender:

> Independently of the internal genitals and independently of the chromosomes. Why? Because this person has identified herself as a woman all her life, and feels she is a woman.
>
> *(Medical class)*

The final defining criterion of gender, then, is in the order of identification. Although equally restricted to sexual bimorphism, it evokes a more psychological or social discourse for the expert criterion, which must examine not just the body, but also the subject's gender ascription. That this ascription may be made "independently of the internal genitals and independently of the chromosomes" shows that the subject's identification does not necessarily develop in line with biological development, but on the contrary may appear to clash with it, the only alternative in a framework of interpretation that limits the options of identification to the excluding boundaries of sexuation.

At this point, we might think that the explanation of transsexuality is based on a psychosocial reading of gender and identity, but the class continues as follows:

> It seems that at 12 weeks – these are some theories that we will discuss – whatever, because it is not very clear what it is, also begins to form, to act on the brain [. . .] Current theories say that it also differentiates, and in these differences, other hormones or other factors act on this brain to masculinise or feminise it [. . .] It would be like a case of intersexuality, but of late onset: when the brain has to differentiate is when it changes route, and that person will therefore be born with chromosomic and genital sex and everything all pointing in one direction, while cerebral sex points in another.
>
> *(Medical class)*

As you can see, we would have been wrong to follow our intuition. Gender identification does not take place at the psychosociological level at all, but in a sort of neural-chemical-anatomical complex. The brain is constructed in a development that is homological with the bimorphic, and heterosexually articulated configuration of the genitalia. It takes us to what Ian Gold and Daniel Stoljar (1999) call *the neuron doctrine*, a dominant idea in cognitive neuroscience that holds that emergent or mental properties, as gender identity is, are high order effects that depend on phenomena of inferior properties.

Presenting the quantitative and evolutionary datum of the 12 weeks reinforces the hegemonic discourses of sexual dualism, reproduces the normative imposition of a linear development, and has the rhetorical effect of speaking of a knowledge that is exact and therefore credible, in an example of what Paul Preciado (2008/2015) calls *somatic fiction*. Fiction of the embryologisation of a prediscursive, ahistorical and organic gender, that may have a linear development since the chromosomes or can change course and *genderise* the brain in a path contrary to that traced by sexual bimorphism. This implies a rupture of the heterosexual evolutionary chain, a fault in the correlation between "chromosomic sex" and "cerebral sex" that refers to a motoring metaphor: a change of route, a sign indicating the possibility of turning off the road – a road supposedly demarcated by biology.

As Silvia García and Carmen Romero (2012) point out, defining transsexuality as a case of intersexuality[5] is a resource often used to legitimise the need for surgical interventions in transsexuality. Thus, interventions on the body are configured as a technical readjustment to correct *errors* or accidents on the road to an intelligible body and subject. Techniques that are justified by the fiction of introducing in the body the models that regulate what it is to be, or feel one is, a man or a woman; discourses that naturalise the social constructions about gender as something proper to bodies (Martínez, 2005). That *late* intersexuality is referred to here only shows the sophistication that science attributes to the brain, whose development is to be found in *later* stages of the embryonic process.

As science researcher Anne Fausto-Sterling (2000) reminds us, one of the cerebral differences between the sexes most mentioned in the literature are the shapes and dimensions of the corpus callosum, a bundle of neural fibres that connects both cerebral hemispheres. Based on a meta-analysis of scientific articles published between 1982 and 1997, the author reveals how these studies have been based on two-dimensional sections of this unifying band, laboratory sections that transform the original object but nevertheless are signified and interpreted as if they were indeed original. Yet, even if we accept their treatment as original objects, the author tells us that no data has consistently indicated the presence of this sexual dimorphism. But even if we accept these claims as demonstrated, would they be sufficient to speak of the direction of their effects, of a masculinisation or feminisation of the brain?

This exercise in interpretation recalls anatomical studies that served in the past to justify differential treatment of ethnic minorities (e.g., Bean, 1906), and are now replicated to justify the reproduction of social inequalities between men and women, by *finding* in the brain, for example, differences of cognition, interests and habits (Gómez, Esteva & Fernández, 2006); or associations between biology and sexual differences in the field of psychopathology (Hirshbein, 2010), and even sexual orientation, which the Dutch Institute of Brain Research associates with differences found between men and women in the size of the hypothalamus (Swaab & Hofman, 1995). The presentation of laboratory findings as evidence of the biological substrata of conducts, identifications or racial differences, as well as of sexual orientation, gender and transsexuality, is necessarily tautological unless the theoretical-epistemological assumptions behind experimentation and the interpretation of its results are made explicit (Bourdieu, Chamboredon and Passeron, 1973/2002). Until then, the only serious *scientific* option is to leave them in suspense while we interrogate their theoretical-political commitments (Longino, 1990; González, 2005).

Where is the psycho-social? Rhetorics of colonisation

In the class we just reviewed, we saw how medical science presents gender identification not as a psychological or social phenomenon but as a product of biology and its changes of route. In order to probe more deeply into the rhetorical articulation between identity and biology, which while appearing to incorporate the psychosocial dimension actually annuls it, let us now turn to another form of scientific divulgation: a book chapter co-authored by gender clinic professionals, dedicated exclusively to exploring the causes of transsexuality. I reproduce here the main titles of its table of contents,[6] which deal with three possible hypotheses for transsexuality:

> Initial and current hypotheses:
>   Psychosocial hypothesis: Money's theory on the influence of learning, or sex by upbringing.
>   Biological hypothesis: disturbance in the process of sexual differentiation.
>   Mixed hypothesis: interaction between biological and environmental factors.
>
> *(Gómez, Esteva & Fernández, 2006, p. 113)*

In speaking of "initial and current hypotheses", the text makes a division between a theoretical past and a scientific present. The first hypothesis considered, the "psychosocial hypothesis", is preceded by the word "initial", implying that it occupies a historical not present position, from which we can suspect that it has been replaced by new theoretical models. This recalls what Celia Kitzinger (1987/1989) calls *up the mountain* rhetoric (frequent in social science publications about lesbianism and male homosexuality), whose function is to "illustrate the superiority of contemporary over past research findings" (Kitzinger, 1987/1989, p. 8). If science constructs itself as continuously improving, then what is not of the present is not only in a temporal past, but above all in a scientific past and is therefore without legitimacy. If we follow this script established by the rhetoric used, the "biological hypothesis" would occupy a present or more present position, defined by the metaphor of the *change of route* or "disturbance in the process of sexual differentiation" that we already discussed. Enjoying even greater scientific legitimacy, we would find the "mixed hypothesis", occupying the opposite extreme to the "psychosocial hypothesis" on the past/present or scientific legitimacy axis. How, then, is it possible to think of a "mixed hypothesis", in a half-rescue of the psychosocial, while at the same time the latter is rhetorically discarded as a plausible or scientific explanation of transsexuality?

It *is* possible, in that the proposal of a mixture between the "psychosocial hypothesis" and the "biological hypothesis" dismantles the psychosocial with a daring substitution of terms. While the reference to biology is maintained in the phrase "biological and environmental factors", the reference to the psychosocial is changed into a reference to environmental factors. Etymologically, the word environmental derives from the Old French *environer* (in English, to surround, enclose, encircle). The psychosocial, then, reduces to being *what surrounds* something else, understood as the centre. Returning to the class, we know that the centre encircled by these non-biological factors is precisely biological or physiological and specifically the brain and its differentiation. The "interaction" that the mixed hypothesis talks about, then, is limited, at the most, to two types of factors that together *act* on the biological (in this case, the brain): one in a relation of interiority (biological factors) and one of exteriority (environmental factors).

Let us look at it another way. What science and the clinic present as a mixed hypothesis would not be possible if the psychosocial includes the sex/gender system (Rubin, 1975), on which 1970s feminism was based and which snatched gender away from biology and psychology; or if it includes the queer critique of the sex/gender system, which suspends the nature/culture divide in the socio-scientific construction of sexed bodies (Wittig, 1992;

Haraway, 1991; Preciado, 2000/2011). Nor would it be possible if it includes the critique of the artificiality of sexual bimorphism (Fausto-Sterling, 1993); the analysis of the normative control of heterosexuality as the obligatory desire (Rich, 1980/2003); or the dismantling of gender as a truth or *expressive* identity (Butler, 2004). The rhetorical inclusion of the psychosocial in the mixed hypothesis is only possible because in reality it does not involve a rescue of the psychosocial at all. The theory representing the psychosocial here is reduced to the interactionist theory of John Money,[7] who conceived the identity or gender role as a product of the communion between biology and what was acquired, and maintained that humans are differentiated by the sexual binomial. This is why this exercise of the supposed rescue of the psychosocial becomes possible, in that neither the dismantling of (cerebral) sexual difference, nor of its biological or natural basis are present. Putting it into the discourse via a mixed hypothesis has a single, clear purpose: to deproblematise the presentation of the biological hypothesis, freeing it from any possible tension to which psychosocial theories could expose it.

Thus, although the psychosocial still appears discursively, it does so displaced to a lower level or subordinated by biology, in whose incidence – one that is only a possibility – it has an explanatory role. It is presented as part of the theoretical model but only as a possible trigger of the brain's sexual differentiation, activating something already contained in the anatomical structure, like a truth waiting to be revealed. In this way, although the mixed hypothesis is presented as including the psychosocial in the understanding of gender and the construct of sexual difference, in reality the psychosocial is subordinated to a bio-bio-bio model, eliminating the psychological and social from the supposed "etiological sandwich" (Baldiz, 2010, p. 150) presented by the rhetoric of *the mixed* or bio-psycho-social. In the words of John Read:

> The term "bio-psycho-social" model [. . .] is more illusion than reality [. . .]. Life events have been relegated to the role of "triggers" of an underlying genetic time-bomb. This is not an integration of models, it is a colonisation of the psychological and social by the biological.
>
> *(Read, 2005, p. 597)*

Gender as hormonal production

While we were reviewing the class and its biological explanation of transsexuality, we saw that the rhetoric of the change of route – as the brain's supposed change of direction in sexual development is represented – is based on the influence of so-called sexual hormones on the foetus and its brain. Reproducing thinking dominated by a neuro-molecular gaze (Abi-Rached & Rose, 2010), or colonisation of subjectivity by neurology and the *psy sciences* (De Vos, 2013), this theory of "foetal programming" (Lombardo et al., 2012) rests on the differential bio-natural production of amounts of oestrogens, progesterone and testosterone of sexed bodies, which could potentially affect the sexes asymmetrically in their future behaviour. It is a question of amounts, finally, even though the socio-scientific language continues to talk of male and female hormones, as if it were a question of molecular products exclusive to one body or the other, as a chemical basis for sexual dimorphism (Hausman, 1992).

As the science researcher Nelly Oudshoorn (1994/2005) reminds us, the female body became the first hormonal laboratory due to the asymmetrical institutionalisation of research, facilitated by hospital circuits in which the scrutiny, monitoring and control of the female body favoured the collection of specimens needed for research. If the female body was reduced to the uterus until the nineteenth century and to the ovaries since the middle of that century, with the rise of sexual endocrinology the reduction shifted to the chemical substances first labelled as hormones in 1905.

In his historical analysis of the contraceptive pill, Paul Preciado (2008/2015) argues that the pharmaceutical industry collaborates in a policy regime of body modification, in which the molecule transmutes into a dispositive for the production and control of gender. The pill, then, is not only a birth control technology although indeed one of demographic regulation from its beginnings when it was tried out, with racial *cleansing* objectives, on black (and homosexual) populations in Puerto Rico (Grant, 1994; Roberts, 1997). In our days, with its entry into the domestic sphere and the massification of its use, the pill appears mainly as a "program for the cosmetic production of femininity" (Preciado, 2008/2015, p. 142). It controls acne, eliminates body hair, reduces weight, improves the appearance of the skin, and produces artificial hormonal cycles (or techno-periods) to imitate the illusion of the natural woman.

This led the philosopher to develop the concept of *bio-drag* or somatic transvestism, a "pharmopornographic production of somatic fictions of femininity and masculinity" (Preciado, 2008/2015, p. 130),[8] in which the *pharmo* refers to the biomolecular techniques for governing sexual subjectivities. Femininity, and in our times masculinity too with the new technologies for the surveillance and control of the penis and erections, both understood as a "domain of capitalization and biopolitical engineering" (Preciado, 2008/2015, p. 126), as centres for the traffic of molecules capable of (re)feminising and boosting masculinity (here the political imbalance in the control of bodies is evident), modulating subjectivities and extending gender performativity to biology itself.

Let us look, then, at how genders or somatic fictions of femininity and masculinity are produced biomolecularly, by focusing on the dispositive of hormone prescriptions as a clinical treatment aimed at gender reassignation. Yes, of gender, and not *just* of sex, not only because "sex, by definition, will be shown to have been gender all along" (Butler, 1990/1999, p. 12), but also because as Ángel Gordo (1995) points out, quoting Judith Shapiro, these clinical techniques "impose the acquisition of behaviours and desires that correspond with their new sexes" (p. 135). The following fragment shows some of the physical and psychological effects associated with the ingestion of so-called female hormones:

> When their breasts start to grow, they show them to you . . . then, with time, they become more, er . . . like they are more, er . . . they are not so upfront, ok? and a bit more reserved. More modest,[9] but at the beginning they are not at all, right? that's curious as well. Like the modesty comes later.
>
> *(Psychologist, interview)*

Breast growth is one of the most notorious physical effects of the continuous ingestion of oestrogen prescribed in combination with testosterone inhibitors. As we know, breasts are a sexually signified space, to which femininity is anchored in a dual function (both of them configured by a heterosexual regime): breastfeeding and therefore maternity, and the sexual attraction of men (Wilkinson & Kitzinger, 1994; Coll-Planas, Alfama & Cruells, 2013). Hormones work, then, not only by relocating body fat in breasts, but also by imitating what they contain as a double feminine presence: maternity and heterosexual intercourse, reflecting a sexual politics that constructs femininity *in* being the object of male sexual-reproductive desire. As a "somatic centre of gender production" (Preciado, 2008/2015, p. 137), these breasts are no more nor less performative imitators than natural breasts, produced by technology, medicalised, pathologised, reconstructed and (nearly always) synthetically hormoned. Feminine subjectivity, then, starts to be modulated together with the body modification: a modulation that works by redirecting looks toward the person and relocating their political position in a space of socio-sexual-naturalised forms.

That "with time, they become [. . .] a bit more reserved" refers precisely to the position of *visibility disguised as invisible* that breasts occupy in the public space (Ussher, 1989). If it is true that they are now "not so upfront" but "more modest", it is the breasts and their socio-cultural meaning that relocate the position of the hormoned body, subjectivating the subject through the need to be a hidden presence – one only suggested for the private enjoyment of another (breastless) body. Molecularly, then, not only a chemical sequence that modifies the body is introduced into it, but also the looks of others, male desire, and the privatisation of a torso that was previously public.

The presentation of the narrative as something "curious" works as a rhetorical resource that safeguards the statement from being understood as a subjective appreciation. It makes the statement "modesty comes later" appear to be a confirmed clinical fact, faced with which any presupposition is suspended. As an example of what Jonathan Potter (1996) calls *stake inoculation*, this works by blocking possible criticism that the statement is a purely subjective appreciation by implying that the facts are so consistent that they overcome any previous idea, and even surprise someone who presents themself as a *modest witness*, able to detach themselves from the cultural context and make an objective observation about reality (Haraway, 1997). The effect is to present modesty as a biological datum, as the consequence of typically female hormones, and thus also as a typical characteristic of women.

Of course, this is not a universal female characteristic but the prescription of sole modes of being that combine with pharmacology to produce a homogenised model of *the woman*. The breast-appropriation of public spaces in some political demonstrations or festivities (think of the photographs of techno-breasts in gay pride marches, or their use as a platform of demands by some feminist groups) contradicts the universalisation of feminine sexual reserve (modesty) and, on the contrary, show how it is socially regulated by vigilance and punishment.[10]

But it's not only a question of modesty. In the technological production of both femininity and masculinity, the limits of biology expand until they contain everything, including emotions and relational patterns:

> In the boys, their self-esteem goes up a lot, they get more, er . . . a touch more aggressive, you know? They seem more irritable, er . . . more defiant, they lose their fear, er . . . they get more critical, more assertive and their sexual activity increases a lot, their libido hits the roof. In the women on the other hand it is different, their libido drops, eh . . . ? Sex for the sake of sex is no longer it . . . they need an emotional bond to have sexual relations.
>
> *(Psychologist, interview)*

Women are not only (re)constructed as lacking in sexual desire, something described often in the literature (e.g., De Cuypere et al., 2005), but also as needing an emotional link to exercise their sexuality. Apart from the anatomical-functional changes the hormones could produce physiologically, decreasing or eliminating erections and libido, they are also presented as regulating sexuality in the field of relations. The narrative of sexuality as anchored in an emotional bond recalls the construction and regulation of female sexual behaviour as undesiring and passive (Laqueur, 1990/2003; Fernández, 1993/2010) that goes back to the Enlightenment and persists to this day, despite the findings of twentieth-century sexology. Sexuality shrinks to fit the space of intimacy, of encounters made possible by trust and permanence, very remote from the stereotype of the prostitute (Espejo, 2009) and very close to the model of the good wife. Transsexual men, on the other hand, would find that hormonation boosts their sexual desire, in a political mechanism that optimises their circulation as sexually desiring and public subjects. This contrast between the two sexed models can be seen more clearly in the following two excerpts, the first from an interview with a transsexual man, and the second with a transsexual woman, both in hormonal treatment:

> You become colder [. . .] it's not that you don't have feelings. Colder, full stop.
>
> *(Rodrigo, FtM, interview)*

> Fierce sensations. Like, sometimes you are speeding and wanting to do things, and then after five minutes you feel like crying, you feel you need a hug, you feel . . . and then you go back again and feel normal, or you feel down, and then you feel up.
>
> *(Miriam, MtF, interview)*

The clinical devices, then, with their therapeutic and biomolecular technologies, before being surgical, form part of a complex technology of gender (De Lauretis, 1987), that produces gender by intervening the bodies of transsexual persons. In reassignation to masculine gender, the chemical doses are described as having the potential to bring to birth sexually active, cold, aggressive, defiant, irritable, fearless, critical, and assertive men. The female gender, by contrast, appears with characteristics of sexual passivity and modesty, instability, tearfulness, and in need of affection. This recalls Jane Ussher's *mad woman* (1989), governed by a supposed inherently unstable biological structure, that is typical of scientific research into menstrual cycles and their behavioural effects. A bio-chemical production, then, of masculinity and femininity. A trans-formation of the body in laboratories in which one or another gender variable is mixed in test tubes to find the formula wanted.

(Ir)reversible bodies

The techno-scientific construction of the feminine, that collage of prostheses, molecules, and emotions, depends also on body-shaping surgery. Vaginoplasty, as a surgical technique, is presented imitating a model based on revealing the feminine within the male body, as the following excerpt shows:

> Imagine a glove, a rubber glove, and you turn it inside out and put it inside, invaginate it. So, from the penis you make a sort of bag that is placed inside and a space is created in the woman, in the man, between the anus and the urethra. The glans, which as you saw before in the embryonic process, the male glans corresponds to the woman's clitoris, is usually retained, with its veins and nerves, in order to form a clitoris from them. So that this person, this woman, can retain sensitivity, have orgasms and enjoy sex. And the cavernous bodies, what is inside the penis, is removed. That is it, in general terms.
>
> *(Medical class)*

In this description of the surgery, the technique is pictured as turning the penis inside out, so that it is like a bag that is placed inside. Discursively, although the technique implies the aesthetic construction of a vulva, there is no mention of the construction of a vagina, but of an invagination, "as if the penis naturally contained the possibility of becoming a vagina" (Preciado, 2000/2011, p. 114). At this technical and linguistic level, femininity is not constructed but is discovered in the male body. As Fausto-Sterling (2000) puts it, "females don't need anything built; they just need excess maleness subtracted" (p. 59). Femininity on the inside, like the correction of a corporal development that ought to tip over toward its inner space.

The "rubber glove" metaphor depicts the reversibility of the male body, recalling constructions of medical knowledge that date from the second century with Galen of Pergamon,[11] who constructed a version of the female body as an inversion of the male in almost the same terms that we now see repeated 19 centuries later. The construction of a female body, then, as an inversion of the male – an operation that does not work in reverse: in clinical terms, the clitoris does not exist ontologically, but is defined as a derivative or a minor antecedent of what *really* exists: the penis. In other words, "femininity corresponds to an irreversible model of the production of sex" while "masculinity is constructed according to a hermaphrodite model that allows the 'natural' passage from the penis to the vagina" (Preciado, 2000/2011, p. 115). Proof of this is the unequal technological development and its precarious prosthetic constructions of the penis, or phalloplasty (carried out with sections of skin and flesh from the female body). Its most common post-operative complications are urethral fissures, pressure injuries (ulcers caused by pressure or inadequate blood circulation), extrusion of the penile or testicular prothesis (ulcers through which the prothesis is exposed externally), urethral-cutaneous fistulas, urethral stenosis (narrowing of the urethra), bladder-vaginal fistulas (communication between the bladder and the vagina) and lithiasis (formation of calculi) in the neourethra (Caballero et al., 2007).

That the feminine appears as contained in the masculine refers us to a clinical-discursive construction in which the feminine occupies a pre-evolutionary or primary space closer to an original model. A body developed by molecular absences, prior to the action of so-called male hormones that would propel its development *one step further*. The woman, then, is discursively constructed as contained within the man (like the biblical rib) or as an inversion of the male body, in a position of evolutionary inferiority, as in a pre-male state. This returns us to the model of the "single sex", which for Thomas Laqueur (1990/2003) is a feature of pre-eighteenth-century scientific development, when anatomical differences were interpreted as hierarchically organised variations on the same model, in which the woman represented the imperfect or unfinished development of the male body.

If "every scientist knows now that biological form *by default* in nature is the female"[12] (Punset, 2007), what is the male then? A perfected version of the female? Does the femininity, then, represent a threat of deterioration? Does that mean that "maintaining masculinity requires *suppression* of the feminine?" (Fausto-Sterling, 2000, p. 204). The construction of the female *by default*, a common rhetoric in the specialised literature, not only refers us to the logic of sexual differentiation, in which the intervention of *male* hormones would produce the outward development of what would otherwise, or by default, remain locked inside the female body (clitoris, ovaries and uterine cavity). Above all, it constructs femininity as potentially contaminating, as an imperfection or defect, as quasi-mutilated when compared to *a unique and perfect* body, faced with which the woman is constructed as otherness.

The double biologisation of gender: biologising the performance

Continuing with the construction not just of the body but above all of gender through medical reassignation technologies, let us see how biologisation operates in regard to gender actions or performances in clinical and medical discourses on transsexuality:

> Man, if you are capable of going out as a woman, I mean, if you, who are a boy, are capable of putting on some earrings, painting your lips and going out on the street, man . . . there is definitely something. And if you also can put on a skirt, there is something more. But, if instead, it's impossible, "how am I going to go out", well ok then, it's more doubtful.
>
> *(Psychiatrist, interview)*

This extract shows, above all, the construction of gender and specifically the construction of a woman, as an imitation based on appearance. The request or mandate, proper to the diagnostic phase, is prescriptive of the feminine as an aesthetic, but one that involves a certain difficulty and for that reason is susceptible to evaluation. To *be capable of*, as a conventional implicature (Grice, 1975), means that not everybody is *capable*, and such a capacity is a symptom that confirms the diagnosis. In other words, the capacity to imitate aesthetically what a woman is would indicate the feminine gender of the person who attends the diagnostic scene.

The interest of the extract is that it shows us a dual vision of what gender and its detection in the body are. On the one hand, "you, who are a boy" refers to the masculine identity, which as such would be in the order of membership, continuity, and the unity of the body involved. On the other hand, "you are capable of going out as a woman" refers to the possibility of not repeating the gender performances defined by identity, and in this very act, it denaturalises what at the same time is anchored in identity as an attribute.

"You, who are" versus "capable of going out as", identity versus imitation; a discursive mixture that, while designating gender as a definition of the body, presents gender with a possibility of discontinuity made concrete in a personal capacity to intervene the body cosmetically. It is the latter that is presented as evidence for the diagnosis: the capacity to perform a gender that is constructed as being opposite to the assigned one. But if we assume that gender identity is a biological fact in the clinical discourse, and that the cause of transsexuality can be found in biology, it follows that this performative *capacity* is itself reduced to a biological condition, to an embryonic maladjustment that would explain the possibility of imitating actions that do not correspond to the gender assigned normatively to the sexed body.

Conversely, when this sign/symptom is not detectable, if the capacity is not present, "if instead, it's impossible", the *crossed* gender ascription or identification (according to dichotomic logic) is placed in question, and therefore the diagnosis is "more doubtful" or is discarded. Hence the importance of these demands for demonstration or diagnostic requirements, as they provide evidence of something that is not directly observable: biology, with its *changes of route*.

In other words, not only is the biologisation of identity performative in its construction of genders as natural, essential, ahistorical and atemporal, but gender as a performance is also biologised. As an effect of the biological discourse of transsexuality, gender is constituted as something contained in neurochemical circuits; anything that may be interpreted as parodic, imitative and even subversive in the continuous acting out of the cultural requisites of gender membership is transformed into a symptom of maladjustment in the supposed chain of events in embryonic development that join the body to the brain. To conduct oneself over a prolonged period like the *other* gender is transformed into a biological sign: dressing in skirts or trousers, using ear-rings or not, using lipstick or not, is something only possible if biology (in disorder) allows it to be.

The foregoing is not part of the same process of biologising identity; it responds to a mechanism of double biologisation. On the one hand, gender identification is biologised; on the other, the capacity to perform gender is also made to be biological. Certainly, if gender is a biological fact, we can assume that this capacity also is, and therefore that this biologisation of per-formance is a discursive redundancy from another clinic moment. However, the discursive effects are different here. To state that our biology determines gender is not the same thing as saying that it also determines the ability to imitate the *other* gender. The first statement – we are men and women because we are so biologically – is well known; feminism has discussed it for more than half a century. But the second is a response to contemporary theories that broadly speaking not only snatch gender from biology, but also lay bare its imitative character. The assertion in this case is that this imitation is also marked by biology, independently of the fact that the assigned gender is itself supported by a whole lifetime of performances, and therefore also on the ability to imitate.

In summary, this double biologisation fulfils the paradoxical function of denaturalising gender (you do not *go out* necessarily as you *are*), by re-natural-ising it (if you *go out* as what you *are not*, it must be because that is what *you are*). This makes identity into a wildcard that anchors us, in whichever of its dimensions and theoretical apprehensions, to our biology. Even if identity is a purely ritualistic repetition of the social norms that construct sexed bodies, it is only that way because biology allows the repetition to be possible and sustainable through time.

Does biologisation psychopathologise?

In legitimating scientific explanations concerning health and what is healthy, not only rhetorical constructions of objectivity (Cabruja & Vázquez, 1995; Potter, 1996) play an important role, but also rhetorical constructions of scientific knowledge as beneficial to our society (Oudshoorn, 1994/2005). To put it differently, what science says shares a status of truth and desirability. The rhetorical production of this effect is what Celia Kitzinger – taking up Jonathan Potter and Michael Mulkay's (1982) concept of a Standard Utility Account (SUA) – calls *utility accounting*, referring to the ways in which research and its progress are presented as being socially useful, as "helping to solve the problems of oppression [...] [and giving an] image of science in the service of suffering humanity" (Kitzinger, 1987/1989, p. 21).

It is interesting, therefore, to trace how biological explanations of transsexuality are presented as socially useful. In the midst of a broad debate on the inclusion of transsexuality in the psychiatric manuals, especially during the years before the appearance of DSM-5,[13] the biological hypothesis we have discussed is presented as having the potential of ridding transsexuality of its psychopathologising connotations. In the following extract from a book on transsexuality co-edited by professionals of the gender clinic, we see an example of the voice of biology in this debate:

> Thus, we are dealing with a process similar to what occurs in cases of intersexuality, in which there are disagreements between chromosomic, and/or gonadal, and/or hormonal, and/or genital sex. Based on this hypothesis proposed by the Amsterdam gender team, a team with long experience of these disorders, transsexuality should not be considered a psychiatric problem per se, just as cases of intersexuality are not considered or included in manuals of mental disorders.
>
> *(Gómez, Esteva & Fernández, 2006, p. 117)*

Just as intersexuality responds to the observation and interpretation of bodily signs as an ambiguity in the sexual truth – that the clinic proposes to *unveil* by means of surgical interventions – so transsexuality is presented as a sort of similar, also organic, ambiguity. This causal theory is legitimised in terms of its scientific origin as being the product of a "team with long experience of these disorders", in an example of the use of a rhetoric of mythologisation of expertise, in which scientists are credited "with access to knowledge denied to ordinary mortals" (Kitzinger, 1987/1989, p. 10).

The factual rhetoric confirming that transsexuality "should not be considered a psychiatric problem per se" is only comprehensible as a dialogic production (Bakhtin, 1986), as a response to questioning of the psychopathologisation of the category. However, in its association with intersexuality, a medicalised and pathologised entity (through which its biological character is emphasised), transsexuality is not snatched from the realm of psychiatry. The expression "per se" plays the role of a disciplinary anchorage, which while locating the cause in something extra-psychiatric, in some way makes it stay within the discipline regarding what that "per se" leaves outside. On the contrary, the association with intersexuality takes it into a wider field of medical specialisation that adds endocrinological and surgical disciplines to the psychological ones. In other words, not only is a causal and ideological connection established between intersexuality and transsexuality, but also a technological one (Hausman, 1992, 1995; Fausto-Sterling, 2000; Balza, 2009). By a sort of displacement, the surgical handling of intersexuality also legitimates interventions on the bodies of persons diagnosed with gender dysphoria.

While biology appears as a response by which the *psy sciences* have de-psychologised the category, as a declaration that "subjectivity is in this way secondary [and] consequently not the place where things *go wrong*" (De Vos, 2013, p. 102, emphasis added), the appearance of the term "disorders", even without its adjective "mental", works by saying that something *has gone wrong*. But if we assume that "biology does not imply a distinction between normal and abnormal function" (De Vos, 2013, p. 98), there would be no reason to maintain that something has gone wrong in transsexuality, nor is there any reason to do so with healthy bodies incorporated under the category of intersexuality. The rhetorical strategy that articulates biologisation with pathology in this excerpt, by naming transsexuality as a disorder, explicitly shows that the *psy sciences* have not abandoned the category. It reveals that biologisation is far from meaning that the discipline has renounced the criteria of normality and abnormality that support its knowledge and practice on gender, and that on the contrary, it works as a rhetoric of scientific objectivation – or scientific transvestism – of its own regulatory operations.

Notes

1 Referring to heterosexuality, Adrienne Rich states:

> this "preference" does not need to be explained unless through the tortuous theory of the female Oedipus complex or the necessity for species reproduction. It is lesbian sexuality which (usually, and incorrectly, "included" under male homosexuality) is seen as requiring explanation. This assumption of female heterosexuality seems to me in itself remarkable: it is an enormous assumption to have glided so silently into the foundations of our thought. (1980/2003, p. 17)

2 Sedgwick, referring to Louis Crompton's concept of *gay genocide*, reminds us that "there is a history of the mortal suppression, legal or subjudicial, of gay acts and gay people, through burning, hounding, physical and chemical castration, concentration camps, bashing" (1990, page 128).

3 After the war, the doctor was received and protected by government of the time in Argentina, where he continued to study his hypothesis of hormonal causes, and to try out more sophisticated techniques of "treatment" (such as implanting hormonal dosing devices), with the support of the Argentine Ministry of Health.

4 A detailed analysis of this class, centred on the rhetorics of objectification in the biological explanations of identity, appeared in Roselló and Cabruja (2012).

5 Until the year 2013, intersexuality was a category that, when present, excluded the diagnosis of what then was called Gender Identity Disorder. In the latest edition of the American psychiatric manual (DSM-5), Gender Dysphoria may appear in coexistence with intersexuality.

6 Each of these titles includes a series of sections or subtitles. The decision not to present them only serves to simplify the presentation of the analysis.

7 In the 1950s, John Money established a protocol for treating intersexuality based on an early surgical intervention (before 18 months), to be hidden for life from the subject intervened and supported by early upbringing in the assigned gender. It was precisely with him, and therefore, with the medical-psychological apparatus, that the concept of gender was born as a reference to the subject's cultural belonging to masculinity or femininity. His theory was widely accepted until the alleged success of his controversial "case" known as John/Joan was exposed for its violence and emphatically refuted by Diamond and Sigmundson (1997).

8 In the words of the author,

> Pharmacopornographic capitalism could be defined as a new regimen of body control and subjectivity production that emerged after World War II, with the emergence of new synthetic materials for consumption and bodily reconstruction (such as plastics and silicone), the pharmacological marketing of endocrine substances to separate heterosexuality and reproduction (such as the contraceptive pill, invented in 1947) and the transformation of pornography into mass culture. (Preciado, 2010, pp. 112–113)

9 In Spanish, the original language of the quotation, the word used was *pudor*, which has no exact equivalent in English. In Spain and most Spanish-speaking countries, the word refers specifically to the shame or embarrassment of showing one's naked body or speaking of matters related to sexuality.

10 Vigilance and punishment that sometimes borders the absurd, as when in January 2017 about 20 policemen were deployed on a beach in Necochea, Argentina, to demand that three female bathers cover their breasts under threat of arrest.

11

> First, imagine with me the [parts] of the man turned inwards and extending inside between the rectum and the bladder; on this assumption, the rectum would occupy the place of the womb with the testicles on each side of the external part; the male's penis will become the neck of the cavity that is produced, and the skin at the end of the penis, which is now called the prepuce, will become the female's vagina. (Galen, quoted in Fernández, 1993/2010, p. 70)

12 This small phrase condenses several rhetorical strategies used to present the stated information as objective. For example, construction of consensus: *all* scientists know now; authorship accreditation: all *scientists* now know, and the rhetoric of accumulated knowledge, or of up the mountain in the order of practices: all scientists *know now* (Kitzinger, 1987/1989, Cabruja & Vázquez, 1995; Potter, 1996).

13 An excellent compilation of works on the depathologisation of transsexuality can be found in Miquel Missé and Gerard Coll-Planas (2010). To review some of the protests and arguments against APA amendments for the category in DSM-5 (prior to its publication) see Jemma Tosh (2011a, 2011b).

3

THE CONFESSED STORY OF UNLIVABLE LIVES

Psychopathologising oppression

Now that we have reviewed how the body is configured, with its functions and desires; the different forms of gender violence implicated in the juridico-clinical interdiscursivity for social recognition; as well as the scientific rhetorics that biologise identity and naturalise heterosexual norms, it is time to propose some ideas about *what* is pathologised and *how* this is done. In other words, to give visibility to the subjectifying effects entailed by the clinical operations and reasons that configure transsexuality as being outside the norms of a healthy life.

To speak of pathologisation is to speak of the constriction of given experiences of life, ways of being or feeling, within a territory of normative regulation, in which medicine dictates "standards for physical and moral relations of the individual and of the society in which he lives" (Foucault, 1963/2003, p. 34). A regulation that in concrete terms takes shape and deploys in and from the clinic, through a knowledge of what is desirable and healthy, of what makes life, or *the* good life, possible, and inversely, of what does not allow it, what makes it more difficult or less desirable.

To speak of psychopathologising is to speak of diverse and complex political technologies of regulation proper to the disciplines of psychiatry and psychology, principally, that work by expanding the subjective limits of persons, of their identities and experiences, through a clinical-interpretative deformation which transforms effects into causes located inside subjects (Rose, 1985, 1989). In this sort of redirection, experiences of distress located in interactive space are psychologised and de-politicised (Cabruja, 2005), translated into deficient or inadequate mental functioning, submitting the individual to the imperatives of a psychological norm that insists on social reproduction (Parker, 2007).

It is an insistence that has been denounced tirelessly, as people from cities across the world turn to the streets every year and every October[1] to denounce that medicine, psychiatry and psychology also make people ill. Demonstrations intensified in the years preceding the publication of DSM-5 (APA, 2013), and among whose consequences was a change that many celebrated: the disappearance of the word "disorder" to denote transsexuality – until 2013 the diagnostic category was "gender identity *disorder*" (APA, 1994) – and its substitution by the term "dysphoria". Allow me not to join this celebration. This lexicon change is above all an addition, given that the category has not abandoned the context in which it was classified: a manual of *disorders*. It is an addition, because now apart from being a disorder, it is a dysphoria as well. I will return to this not-so-new concept in a moment, but first I will pause to look at the semantic and rhetorical effects of transsexuality's continuing anchorage in the empire of mental *disorders*.

In the field of health, the term "disorder" means "an illness that disrupts normal physical or mental functions" or "a minor health disturbance".[2] If we return to the not-so-old conceptualisation of transsexuality as "gender identity disorder" and trace the footprints of its current configuration, we have at least two options of interpretation: that there are gender identities that are healthy and those that are not (with a criterion of *normal* functioning as the reference), or, alternatively, that gender identity could provoke illness or a (minor) health disturbance.

However, this not the only possible meaning of the concept: there is a second meaning associated with regulated conduct. Disorder is also "the breakdown of peaceful and law-abiding public behaviour". So we might think of the concept of disorder at least as occupying an ambiguous space. On the one hand, it places gender identity in the field of health, linking transsexuality to its disturbance. On the other hand, it refers to a breakdown of public or social order. This takes us back to the institutionalisation of the power of psychiatry as hygiene of the social body (Foucault, 1961/2006), as a dispositive for protection and control by means of the double codification of the *undesirable* and *the abnormal*, in which what it carved out as its field of knowledge – sickness and social danger – coalesce (Vásquez, 2012).

The prescription of distress

As I have already mentioned, the removal of the word "disorder" added the term dysphoria to the category, restoring a nomenclature first coined in 1973 by Robert Fisk: Gender Dysphoria. Its inclusion reinforced something the psychiatric institution had highlighted insistently as a diagnostic criterion for the category: distress. As a symptom, this was now converted into an undifferentiable attribute of gender when it does not correspond to that originally assigned, locating the distress not in the problematics or relational consequences of transsexuality but in the gender itself.

Distress has been one of the central criteria for the diagnosis since the appearance of DSM-IV (APA, 1994), whose criterion D stated, "the disturbance causes clinically significant distress or impairment in social, occupational or other important areas of functioning" (p. 538), situating the agency of distress in the disorder or disturbance (this is the lexical substitution). In DSM-5 (APA, 2013) it is criterion B which states, "the condition is associated with clinically significant distress or impairment in social, occupational or other important areas of functioning" (p. 453). As we can see, the descriptions in both editions are practically identical except for two aspects: "disturbance" is replaced by "condition", which is less stigmatising, and the disorder's causative role in the production of distress fades into an association.[3] But what I want to emphasise is an exercise that recurs in both editions – including the intermediate version, DSM-IV-TR (APA, 2002) – and which reflects a discursive polyphony in regard to distress. The conjunction "or" in criterion D in DSM-IV (APA, 1994) or B in DSM-5 (APA, 2013), separates two factors *caused by*, or *associated with* the diagnostic category: on the one hand, clinically significant distress, and on the other, an impairment in social, occupational or other important areas of functioning. The polyphony increases if we include the different usages of the conjunction "or", that is, equivalence, alternative or contrasting terms.

Provoking a quasi "rhetorical use of vagueness", or use of global and vague formulations whose generality makes them difficult to challenge (Potter, 1996), let me translate "clinically significant distress" as a symptom that is detectable in the subject in terms of anxiety, sorrow or pain,[4] and "impairment in social, occupational or other important areas of functioning", as difficulties in the sphere of social and relational life. This ambiguity or vagueness of the psychiatric discourse does not make it explicit whether the distress it establishes as essential to the category circulates from and to the person's interior, or whether it originates in the social environment the person inhabits. If anxiety, sorrow or pain, like all our affective and emotional life, are closely related to our experience of being in a relation with others, and therefore to our social life, their narrative separation from "impairment in social, occupational or other important areas of functioning" contains the discursive possibility of dichotomising them and indeed of obviating one of the two.

Before continuing, I should perhaps point out that this radicalisation of the difference between the two elements of the diagnostic criterion is not an attempt to counter-pose social causes or cultural discursive constructions to subjective emotional states, as if bodies could be isolated from the social environment. The intention, rather, is exactly the opposite: to visibilise that there is no borderline zone between subjectivities, social discourses, and relational spaces; that bodies are constructed through multiple languages that do not deny their materiality, but do bring complexity to their interpretations and their possibilities of inhabitability (Butler, 2004). Ultimately, that it is the psychiatric-psychological rhetoric that discursively constructs a boundary with limited possibilities for transit, and that speaking of causes, origins or explanations of certain experiences acts within a dominant programme of (ab)normalisation, marginalisation and regulation of the social (Sedgwick, 1990) through interventions aimed at peoples' supposed interiority.

This encounter or disencounter between the two dimensions in which distress can be traced analytically does not have a simple solution but a multiple one. It is frequent to find an operation that creates a dichotomy between the relational and what is, in some way, contained by a body understood as a barrier with the environment, in which the experience of a "clinically significant distress" is distinguishable and potentially separable from the social discourses that make possible the inhabitability of bodies and contexts. Locating the conflict *inside* transsexual persons, as persons who are incapable of compatibilising their (gender) identity and their bodily characteristics, is a good example. When transsexuality is conceptualised as a conflict of *appearance*, a dichotomy is created between what are understood socially to be correct and intelligible bodies according to gender norms, and personal valuations of different body parts. Situating the conflict of transsexual persons in bodily acceptance is an exercise of psychologisation that does not problematise the cultural meanings that are forcibly tied to representations and experiences of corporality, which are precisely what make it impossible for the body to be appropriated as desirable and acceptable.

The following extract is an example of the foregoing, where the conflict appears to be situated in a private space or in a sort of disencounter between subjectivity and the body image shown in the mirror:

> There was a time, when I began to go out as a girl, that I was saying my worst enemy is myself. My worst enemy is me in the mirror when I look at myself, and it's like a fight against yourself.
>
> *(Isabel, MtF, interview)*

In this construction of the body as an image the person is split, in a sort of contradictory recognition of corporality. It evokes Lacan's mirror stage (1936/2001), but not to tell us that there was a fault in access to language and the symbolic that allows this demarcation of the body through the image and subsequent sexual identification; rather, it could be interpreted as a symbolic recognition of an already culturally signified body that the subject has appropriated ("*I am* in the mirror"), although apprehended as being in contradiction with her own desire or with an identification not governed by the heteronormative regulations that establish coherence between genital/bodily artifices and sexual membership. The disencounter then, may be displaced from intra-psychic processes (identifications and capacities or failures of symbolisation or repression) to the cultural meanings of the body and its image, to a space in which one's own subjectivity is made possible and constricted, but not necessarily determined.[5]

In other cases, distress appears to be constructed as an experience situated in a link between subjectivities, in an interactive space that is mediated by constraining social norms, by dominant social discourses that make recognition by others impossible. A lack of recognition that is suffered, subverted or challenged, but that located in society and social relations allows a displacement of distress as the axis of the transsexual category (nosological or identitarian), as the following excerpt shows:

> For me, the problem I have is not finding a job; not finding a job I feel crushed, stressed out, and irritable, and then I find myself within the four walls of my house, because I have no job, no money, and I can't go out. So I have an anxiety and that has to be treated, but that doesn't mean I'm ill, it's simply because society hasn't yet assimilated what transsexuality is.
>
> *(Miriam, MtF, interview)*

At the end of this quote, pronounced by a transsexual woman in clinical treatment, distress is presented as the effect of the (dis)encounter between transsexuality and society, the latter being its agent. The excerpt alludes to the socially dominant discourses on gender and sexes and more specifically to their concretely oppressive effects on the lives they conceptualise. Distress, here, appears as constructed as a conflictive valuation of personal experiences, as a consequence of the subject positions (Davies & Harré, 1990) in which social recognition situates certain experiences or identities. The axis of distress is displaced to and located in forms of social violence aimed at these bodies, although with effects of subjectivation or affliction directed at the person's interiority: "I have an anxiety and that has to be treated". Reflecting a "collective consciousness of pathological phenomena" (Foucault, 1963/2003, p. 28), these effects are conceptualised as treatable diagnoses (stress, anxiety), resituating them in an individualising and self-regulating turn that is characteristic of the discipline of psychology (Rose, 1989, 2007; Hook & Parker, 2002; Cabruja, 2013). But although a dominant discourse is reproduced in which distress is psychologised and specialised ("I have an anxiety and *that has to be treated*"), here it is possible to provoke the emergence of a discourse that questions treatment at the individual level of problematics that are located in social relations. Anxiety is presented as the effect of unemployment and economic insecurity,[6] raising to the surface a discourse that links body and material conditions, subjectivity and social positions.

This questioning of the transsexuality-distress link, mediated by oppressive normativities and their daily effects, now not produced by the category, and where the symptom is more a sign of social and labour exclusion, is a somewhat uncommon analytical operation. Rather it is common to find ambiguities in the description of a distress brought into the interior of people, where its origin and direction is confused, but the effect is, as a rule, to psychologise and make more precarious the experience of transsexuality itself as a totalising category.

Of course, the clinic is not unaware of the social violence that affects transsexual bodies, but it deforms the experience and relocates it to the subjects' interiority. Allow me to illustrate the complexity of these relocations with another example, a clinical response to the question, "the suffering is *for being* transsexual?"

> In some cases as well, no? But . . . I mean, it's not a suffering from the beginning, right? It's "what's happening to me?" first, no? "what's happening to me, if a have a body like this and I feel this way".
>
> *(Psychologist, interview)*

"In some cases as well" opens the possibility of a suffering that is disconnected from social experiences, but the statement "it's not a suffering from the beginning" redirects us to an understanding of the latter as an experience within a social context, as non-existent outside our constitution as subjects *in* and *through* relations with others. Although at first glance appearing to be an ambiguity, this operates in fact like a sophisticated rhetoric that has the effect of introjecting in the subject social phenomena and manifestations of violence that the clinic knows and recognises. This is what the extract tells us; the question is returned to the clinical subject by means of a reflexive grammatical construction. "What's happening to me, if a have a body like this and I feel this way" implies that what is occurring has a place *in* the subject, so that the body and the way persons feel are the questioned problematic.

In other words, the phrase "what's happening to me", transposed to a clinical interview, could translate into the question "what is happening to you?" Through this gesture, the experiences that are part of living in a social and cultural world are translated into a reality contained within the person, a reality redirected to the form in which the person experiences and lives their own body and feelings. In Foucault's terms (1976/1978), this is a scientific operation that implies a whole process by which the social is individualised through a ritual of confession, the core practice of psychiatry and psychology, and almost its only medium for performing its diagnoses and clinical histories.

I confess, therefore I exist

> The confession is introduced by the Inquisition in its judicial rites and from there it passes to lay courts. In a context of laicism it passes from judicial rites to scientific techniques: it invades pedagogy and medicine, but also everyday life [. . .] Whoever makes a confession is modified in essence: saved, or cured.
>
> (Ibáñez, 1979/2003, p. 121)

If psychiatric diagnostic manuals are the main reference for clinical descriptions and observations, we can imagine (if the experience and its memory are unavailable) that the staging involved in the diagnostic process as a moment of questions and answers implies actualising and reproducing the criteria that define each category. As we saw recently, these criteria and symptoms, which must be visible to the *expert*, imply the individualising requirement of a personal story focussed on body and feeling.[7] What in reality is a hybrid knowledge (Preciado, 2004) comprising multiple cultural knowledges that give meaning to one's own corporality and identifications, is reinterpreted here by knowledge authorised as expert as a confessed inner truth, making of the conflicting valuations an (almost exclusive) production of the subjectivity of the subject interpellated in the clinical interview.

The subject is not the one who knows about himself despite being the one who is talking; knowledge is on the side of the person listening and who apparently, does not know; the effects, nonetheless, fall on the confessant. Here precisely is where sexuality and its truth emerge, in the intersection and adjustment between the techniques of the confession and scientific discourses, in the structuring of a "confessional science" (Foucault, 1976/1978, p. 64), that makes the subject speak, that interprets and disfigures the narrative (Butler, 2010) into a discursive-scientific web whose main effect is the medicalisation or therapeutic encryption of what has been confessed.

This operational rite of the confession as a central element of clinical practice is at the surface of the following extracts:

(I) If you ask them, "has that made you suffer?" they tell you, "yes". If you ask them "if you don't change, would you suffer? Would you be unhappy?" "Yes".

(II) I ask them a lot if the people around them realised, so sometimes . . . when they say the people around them haven't realised, it's more doubtful. When they say, "yes, other kids noticed that we were different", it's always a support.

(Psychiatrist, interview)

The first of these quotations (I) refers to the evaluation of distress, which as we have seen is constituted as the central element in the diagnosis of transsexuality. The two questions posed, "has that made you suffer?" and "if you don't change, would you suffer? Would you be unhappy?" refer to temporalities (past and future) that cannot be the object of direct observation, as facial expression or any other non-verbal conduct could. The same happens in the second of the extracts (II), where an apparently routine question of diagnostic evaluation also refers us to a temporality (the past) that is not observable. But what these two quotations have most in common is that they refer to two core elements of a diagnosis of transsexuality, which is a key step and the first requirement for gaining access to the chain of health services included in the assistance protocol for transsexual persons: distress and a coherent life history.

The first fragment (I) takes us back to the axis already discussed: transsexuality as an identity associated with distress. The diagnostic criteria that stipulate it work by prescribing what needs to be investigated for the clinical verdict to be given. This is explicit in DSM-5, which restricts the diagnosis to the identification of distress by pointing out that "there must also be evidence of distress about this incongruence" (APA, 2013, p. 453).[8] It is an act with directive illocutionary force (Austin, 1962; Searle, 1969/2011) that gives the category the properties of an object, making it visible and intelligible by indicating, in great detail, what the evaluator must do, see and consider (Martínez-Guzmán & Iñiguez-Rueda, 2010).

These diagnostic criteria, that construct, prescribe and objectify the category, work by structuring the scene of clinical interlocution by means of a specific request for a particular narrative. They form part of a discursive construction of individualised experiences directed at the single individual present in the interview situation, in which the question "has that made you suffer?" demands a response that brings together a whole possible set of relational experiences of violence and of normative oppression, in a sentiment or an affliction that is proper to the person, and confessable. "If you don't change, would you suffer?" directs the suffering toward a state *of* the person, modifiable *in* the person, in an explicit exercise of desocialisation and normative regulation of genders and bodies, which acts by depoliticising the experiences of distress and legitimating the social constructions that determine them.

The second quote (II) brings to mind a predefined and almost mechanised interrogation scene ("I ask them a lot") about a past of experiences and reactions of the "people around them". It implies an assumption of coherence in the life history that expects, and therefore demands, a statement about the first signs of being "different", a difference if not total, at least almost original. If this demand is not satisfied, the diagnosis and, with it, access to the technological assistance protocols for body modification are placed at risk ("it's more doubtful"). It refers us to something that is not stated explicitly in the list of symptoms in DSM-5 (although it is in the description of the course of the "disorder"),[9] related to the time at which what is intended to be diagnosed would have begun to be expressed. It alludes to the distinction between the two variants of transsexuality described by Robert Stoller (1985), the psychiatrist and psychoanalyst who formulated the concept of "essential gender identity": a primary one, implying the child's inability to differentiate itself from the mother's body, and a secondary one, in which *signs* of the assigned gender have been expressed throughout life, mainly in infancy. Although both cases are susceptible to receiving the diagnosis, evidence of so-called primary transsexualism is what facilitates the diagnosis ("it's always a support"), revealing a discourse that naturalises transgender identities by placing the diagnostic truth in an indeterminate space of gender essentialism traced back to the first stages of childhood, or even to the foetal stage, as we saw in the second chapter.

If "evidence" of distress is required to conduct the diagnosis, as well as life stories that are coherent with what the medical discourse constructs as gender dysphoria, and we conclude that the medium par excellence to obtain them is the staging of a confession ritual, then a specular relation between confession and reality is created, which hides the desocialising process implied precisely in the construction of psychiatric reality through the confession ritual.

Clinical histories that are required as evidence for the confirmation of the diagnosis are well known to transsexual persons. The literature has broadly described the adjustment of their narratives to the criteria that will support the obtainment of the diagnosis (an essential certification to initiate the desired medical protocols), such as:

> Infantile episodes of gender confusion, a desire to dress like the opposite sex, absence of sexual excitement when cross-dressing, not having practiced homosexuality in the sex of origin, expressing a strong desire for self-mutilation to eliminate the genitals or secondary sex characteristics, self-identifying as belonging to the other sex, etc.
>
> *(Soley-Beltrán, 2005, p. 212)*

This is what can give rise to a proliferation of stories that are coherent with a medical discourse that not only operates by "rewarding compliance with surgery and punishing honesty with an unfavourable evaluation" (Billings & Urban, 1982, p. 273), but also by configuring – by means of a chain of pathologising linguistic actions – the confession and ascription (at least virtual or strategic) of unitary and coherent identities that are necessarily fastened to an axis of distress.

The following quotation provides an example:

> With the first interview, I got the message. I said, "Now I'm going to have to tell a lie". With the first interview, you realise who the psychologist is.
>
> *(Lucia, MtF, interview)*

The adjustment or performance of these confessions, which the most reactionary literature on transsexuality interprets as a "transsexual fraud" or even as a "perverse montage" (Frignet, 2000/2003), is none other than an adjustment to normative regulations that demand the erasure of everything that makes ascription to one sex or the other ambiguous, both in current practices as in the reconstruction of the past. As Isabel Balza (2009) points out, "transsexual subjects have no choice; if they want surgical help they must submit to the dimorphic and heterosexual system. Otherwise they will be rejected as unsuitable subjects for intervention" (p. 250).

The (psychoanalytic) expression *perverse montage* – which describes a diadic relation in which one of the subjectivities finds itself annulled by the other member of the pair and ends up limited to being a simple object for whatever use the other demands (Frignet, 2000/2003) – actually reveals the workings of a *perverse psychology* (Tosh, 2014). It is not an instrumentalisation of the medical professionals by transsexual persons, but a clinical montage that prescribes and annuls the subjectivity of the persons treated by the clinic. The discursive directives of the protocols conducted by expert, and therefore authorised, voices regulate the reproduction and indeed the acquisition of coherent, unitary and suffering identities, identities that are constructed as previous or original, stemming from a sort of primary development process (Gordo, 1995). It refers to the obligatoriness of a specular response on the part of the subject being clinically interrogated in terms of the diagnostic criteria described in the category, to the need for the narratives to be adjusted to psychiatric knowledge, "thus showing that the medical account is true" (Fernández, 2010, p. 188) – to a *performance of transsexuality*, in so many words (Soley-Beltrán, 2005). It involves a sort of demand to place oneself under the eye of the other, to put oneself at the service of his prescriptive possibility, to constitute oneself as an object of scrutiny – or what comes to the same thing, to deprive oneself of the possibility of agency in one's own definition and construction, to not be (enabled to be) *the witness* of one's own life.

Mental health under suspicion

In the section devoted to comorbidity, DSM-5 (APA, 2013) points out that "clinically referred adults with gender dysphoria may have coexisting mental health problems, most commonly anxiety and depressive disorders" (p. 459). If the verbal form used (may have) implies a possibility that the clinic should be alert to and therefore explore, why does the scientific literature frequently point out that the mental health of transsexual persons is the same as the general population? (e.g., Colizzi, Costa & Todarello, 2014; Gómez, Vidal-Hagameijer & Salamero-Baró, 2008; Gómez-Gil & Zubiaurre-Elorza, 2012). How are these two scientific *truths* articulated? To throw light on this question, let us review a fragment from the interview with one of the researchers from the gender clinic:

> It can be said that a priori, their mental health, if it weren't for the emotional repercussions it produces in them, must be or should be the same as in the general population [. . .] They have normal levels of anxiety, depression, social phobia on average, eh? On average. Why? because they are already in process . . . of course, depending on what moment in their lives you give them this questionnaire, it would turn out totally different. There are people who have never come, who don't know that the possibility exists to, they are surely much worse.
>
> *(Researcher, interview)*

Perhaps the key to approaching this narrative fragment lies in the expression "a priori". If we follow the sequence of the words, it refers to a moment before "the emotional repercussions it produces in them". The causal attribution of the distress implied by use of the verb *produce* need not detain us – I have commented on it previously – but it is striking how the expression "a priori" evokes a scene prior to "the emotional repercussions" (distress) which are nevertheless constructed in close association with the diagnostic category of gender dysphoria. It locates health in a fictitious and impossible past (as if transsexuality could be prior to itself), given that, as we have seen, the psychiatric rhetoric depicts distress as chained and tightly linked to the category, and indeed indissociable from it.

But perhaps more striking is the twist that follows. If transsexual persons have similar levels of anxiety, depression and social phobia to the general population "because they are already in process", then the indicators evaluated as adequate for mental health are also located in a scene in the future, or subsequent to "the emotional repercussions" which before marked a limit with a time in the past or an "a priori" situation. That is to say, this new declaration of a healthy mental state locates the reason for health in the process of undergoing the medical protocol.

In other words, only an impossible transsexuality that is either prior to itself as a psychiatric category, or is under medical treatment, is in the axis of health; a boundary with the "general population" is thereby constructed (in a ı exercise that itself implies dichotomising between transsexual persons and the rest) that only the clinic is able to cross. In this description of the subjects on one side of the boundary or the other, psychiatry not only produces health, but above all determines and regulates experiences of life according to the (socially infiltrated) medical maxim of health (Foucault, 1963/2003; Rose, 1985, 1989, 2007).

The purpose of this analysis of the medical and psychological assertion that the experience of transsexuality does not imply deficient mental health is not to claim that an association between transsexuality and mental illness does exist, but on the contrary, to give sense to these linguistic constructions that hinder a reading of what medical science constructs with this diagnostic category. The mental health of persons defined as transsexuals is not only placed under suspicion but is also constructed as lacking with respect to temporalities that exceed the therapeutic present, in a process of subjectivation that pushes them outside the boundaries of *normality*. Perhaps it is only necessary to add, for the time being and in order to accentuate a peculiarity of the category, that persons who reach the first diagnostic stage of the medical protocols activated by the gender clinic are subjected to extended psychopathological tests.[10] This is a procedure that is only carried out on the hospital admittance of these *patients*; as a general rule it is not applied to any other person who enters the diagnostic machinery, unless a gender identity disorder, gender dysphoria or transsexuality is suspected.

Other psychologisations: social phobia

Obsessive-compulsive, avoidant or borderline personality disorders or traits; adjustment disorders and social phobia; and symptoms of anxiety and depression are some of the most common co-diagnoses. In what follows I will focus on the diagnosis of social phobia, which I consider another striking example of the individualisation and psychologisation of oppression by distorting, as in the construction of distress, effects into causes located inside subjects.

In the following quotation, the expression "many times we see" reminds us of that capacity of medical science of constructing what it has described and constituted, as if it were an original observable in the person, present even before its discursive configuration (Foucault, 1963/2003):

> Many times we see, er . . . that a certain social phobia appears, you know? Because of the way in which society responds to these patients. Fear, fear that people may do them harm, fear of rejection.
>
> *(Psychologist, interview)*

The social phobia that "appears" is a diagnostic category instituted officially by the APA in 1980 with the third edition of the DSM (DSM-III), and which has undergone some changes in later editions. The chapter of DSM-5 (APA, 2013) devoted to anxiety disorders, in which the nomenclature is changed to Social Anxiety Disorder (a change already announced in DSM-IV), states that "the essential feature of social anxiety disorder is a marked, or intense, fear or anxiety of social situations in which the individual may be scrutinized by others" (Criterion A), and that "the social situations almost always provoke fear or anxiety" (Criterion C) (p. 203).

By using the verbs *is* and *provoke*, the linguistic forms of both statements (which have both assertive illocutionary force – a state of things is presented as real – and declarative illocutionary force – in that the enunciatory context, the diagnostic manual, is what publishes and *declares* social phobia to be a disorder), construct the disorder as a concrete, visible entity, specifying the features and effects that must be tracked by the diagnostic procedures.

Just as in the quotation, the fear or anxiety response caused by "social situations" translates into a symptom, into the observable sign of a person who from then on will be the object of a clinical operation of pathologisation. The "marked, or intense, fear or anxiety" despite the recognition of its origin in social violence ("fear that people may do them harm, fear of rejection") is transformed into a problem contained *in* the individual, susceptible to clinical treatment.

"Fear" and "anxiety", declared as observable and symptomatic (always through a confession ritual) will give way to the verdict the diagnosis implies, despite its qualitative coherence with social violence. It is the same individualising shift of the discipline as described previously in relation to experiences of distress: a recognition of violence, of the protection, avoidance and pain responses, at the same time as an isolation in the body, a depoliticisation and psychologisation of the experience of violence.

Together with this process of psychologising normative oppressions, the discipline bases itself on two assumptions for the psychopathological classification of fear. Apart from changing the nomenclature, DSM-5 (APA, 2013) also made a change in the symptomatic description of the diagnosis. The present E criterion states that "the fear and anxiety is out of proportion to the actual threat posed by the social situation and to the sociocultural context" (p. 203), substituting the C criterion of DSM-IV (APA, 1994) for the same diagnosis, which indicated "the person recognizes that the fear is excessive or unreasonable" (p. 417). By tracking the footprints of the diagnosis back in time, we might interpret the expression *out of proportion* as introducing a quantitative norm, and another that is qualitative and mediated by reasonableness, to describe the fear experienced by the subject.

The criterion of unreasonableness, now absent (or concealed) behind an evaluation of inadequate proportions, formerly required a stimulus that was consistent and coherent with a *reasonable* fear. In a disciplinary imposition of emotional regulation, a limit was established between the healthy and the pathological that depended on rational assessments of the fear source. But if here the fear source lies in stigmatisation, discrimination, violence, inequality and isolation, then its recognition implies a normed evaluation of its qualitative consistency with the emotional response, a response that is not susceptible to psychopathologisation given its link with a source that *would deserve* this reaction of/in the subject, so to speak. The diagnosis, then, must be supported by the second of the assumptions that the discipline formerly established for the pathologising of fear: excess.

This quantitative criterion, instituted without details other than the semantic meaning of "excess" (disproportion) in relation to a measure, or to the possibility of measurement, refers to a clinical norm regarding appropriate emotional intensities, or limits, as it were, to what is *quantitatively* healthy.

In order for "the fear that they may do them harm, the fear of rejection" to be psychopathologisable, converted into a symptom, there must be a negative evaluation based on a norm regulating the quantity, strength, intensity or expressivity of the emotion (fear).

What is more, to make the diagnosis possible this norm must be contained in the subject and available to the subject for their own regulation. This is because, returning to the third criterion of DSM-IV, we are told that "the person *recognizes* that the fear is excessive or unreasonable". Even though DSM-5 removed this requirement explicitly, it did so by arguing that persons *might not be capable* of evaluating the norm of excess or disproportion appropriately, making it the clinic's job to assess this adequately.[11] It continues to require, therefore, a kind of self-diagnosis – in which the subject not only must recognise that the stimulus is, or is not, consistent with their fear, but also must evaluate their fear according to a criterion of quantity – but now the diagnosis becomes possible even when the subject's testimony or confession denies any disproportion, thereby resisting that their fear be pathologised.

Self-regulation continues, in that the subject is expected to not *overestimate* the proportion of their fear or anxiety; to demonstrate that the norm has been psychologised and the emotion desocialised. The subject, with their attention on themself, is expected to modulate health-consciously their ways of feeling and being and confess it. This refers us to health practices that inundate everyday life even outside their specific spheres of application, structuring and transmitting adequate ways of being a person (Cabruja, 1998; Hook & Parker, 2002; Parker, 2007), in which subjects must "act upon themselves in the name of their mental health" (Rose, 2007, p. 110).

The construct of social phobia, then, implies not only the existence of adequate emotional reactions and inadequate ones; that there is a health norm in this respect; that the subject must recognise this norm or the expert professional must impose it if this recognition is absent or resisted, but also that the problem is redirected, put inside the subject, based on a quantitative regulation of fear, which is always liable to be "out of proportion", normalising violence by pathologising its effects. By means of the confession as a technique and quantity as a pathologising rhetoric, it becomes possible to individualise and psychologise the effects of a social phenomenon like transphobia – a term that in itself also implies a similar psychologising turn of social violence. A social violence that, according to Sancho (2005), can be expressed principally in five dimensions: social stigmatisation, social discrimination, physical and verbal violence, legal inequality, and social isolation.

A process of individualisation through which, on the one hand, the dangerous consequences of crossing the rigid boundaries dividing genders are denied, while on the other hand their logic of strict demarcation is reinforced by means of the regulations implied by the re-assignation procedures. According to a norm of healthy and pathological quantities, violence is discursively subtracted from violence, in that its effect is constructed in terms of the possibility of emotional disproportion.

For the clinic, transphobia appears as if it had limited effects, less in quantity to those of disproportion; capable of provoking fear but not of constraining the subject within the normative boundaries of gender. Its effects are converted into deficient psychological functioning and this is what is held responsible for the suspension or the impossibility of performing gender when it is not the assigned one. Transphobia as the repressive police of gender (Gordo, 1995; Coll-Planas, 2010a) is depoliticised; it is converted into something inoffensive beyond an almost ritualistic and episodic fear, while its devastating emotional effects are pathologised.

The discursive bond between diagnosis and treatment

At this point, I ask you to accompany me on an analytical journey by examining a short narrative extract that condenses several of the aspects already addressed in this book. The quotation is as follows:

> A person who is transsexual, if not treated, will be bad their whole life. Of course [. . .] Because a person cannot live, cannot live with something that they don't feel is their own.
>
> *(Psychiatrist, interview)*

The grammatical construction of the first part of this fragment ("a person *who is* transsexual") implies that life experiences conceptualised under the category of "transsexual" have a certain homogeneity, a comprehensive characterisation that allows reference to the subjects subjectified under this category without further specification being necessary. It refers to a supposedly shared framework of meaning in which psychiatric nosology is presented as entirely sufficient. Quite clearly, it tells us that transsexuality is an identity to which, as we have seen, psychiatry assigns a specific quality: distress ("will be bad their whole life"). But not only that: it also anchors therapy to the life it conceptualises – "*if not* treated" implies that transsexuality is something that *is treated*, on which the wellbeing of the persons defined by the category is made to depend.

This construction of transsexuality as anchored to a treatment whose *healing power* is determined by the structural link between transsexuality and

treatment, reduces transsexuality to the transit to (and through) medical protocols that can potentially put an end to the subjects' classification by their
psychiatric-medical, and hence psychopathological, identification. Using the
expression of Monstrey and Hoebeke (2003), a potential *de-transsexualising*
capacity is attributed to ideal surgical techniques, which, by sexually reassign-
ing the subject would make their diagnosis disappear (which as we have seen
would, by definition, improve health). In the words of one of the transsexual
persons who are users of the clinic:

> I'll be transsexual until the day they send me for surgery.
>
> *(Isabel, MtF, interview)*

As a diagnostic requirement, the DSM has repeatedly shifted the position of
interventions in the body. Their first appearance was in criterion B of DSM-
III (APA, 1980), which referred to the "wish to be rid of one's genitals and to
live as a member of the other sex" (p. 263). DSM-IV (APA, 1994) eliminated
them as a formal criterion, displacing and limiting the aspiration for interventions to being an orientation for the diagnosis included in criterion B,[12]
referring to distress. DSM-5 (APA, 2013) displaces interventions once more,
converting them into two of the six possible indicators of criterion A, which
refers to a "marked incongruence between one's experienced/expressed gender and assigned gender":

> Criterion A.2: A strong desire to be rid of one's primary and/or sec-
> ondary sex characteristics because of a marked incongruence with
> one's experienced/expressed gender.
>
> Criterion A.3: A strong desire for the primary and/or secondary sex
> characteristics of the other gender.
>
> *(APA, 2013, p. 452)*

Central in the DSM-III diagnosis, as signs of distress in DSM-IV, and as
indicators of gender *incongruence* in DSM-5, treatments are part of the psychiatric category's discursive framework. Despite changes in the language or the
order of the criteria's formal delineation, the manual continues to legitimise
the continuity of this peculiar dialogue between diagnosis and treatment and
ensures that the one is adjusted to the other.

Even more important, the person is made to be responsible for the definition and course of their *treatment*. The statements "*a strong desire to be rid* of
one's primary and/or secondary sex characteristics" and "*a strong desire for* the
primary and/or secondary sex characteristics of the other gender" imply that
the person is constructed not just as the owner and definer of their diagnosis –

insofar as the operation of the confession has disfigured the whole system of sociocultural meanings, and made it into a truth contained in the body and declared by the subject – but also as the source of their treatment. Diagnosis and its treatment are made to coincide as if they originated in the subject, representing medicine both as a simple technology of adjustment, provided to satisfy the subject's demand, and as innocent in its scientific response or offer of a treatment that closes off for the transsexual(ised) person any question that could arise.

Adding to the complexity of this relationship between diagnosis and treatment, the last edition of the DSM (APA, 2013) includes a specifier for the diagnosis that casts doubt on remission of the diagnosis once the reassignment treatments have been achieved, making of transsexuality an (id)entity *in search of* and *in transit through* treatments that nevertheless offer no potential of a "cure". The instructions for the use of the specifier indicate:

> The posttransition specifier may be used in the context of continuing treatment procedures that serve to support the new gender assignment.
> *(APA, 2013, p. 453)*

This implies a totally novel situation in the category's diagnostic guidelines. For the first time, this manual includes the possibility of establishing the diagnosis even when the subject has already undergone medical interventions, by means of a specifier that allows the assignment to be continued. This throws doubt on the construction of the psychiatric (and identity) category as a transitory state or path toward a gender that is culturally intelligible, made possible by medical technologies, after which it would no longer have any sense. It implies a category that is stable in time despite the implementation of *treatments* aiming at anatomical modifications or imitation of the representational image of the sexes, but not at superseding the psychiatric diagnosis.

The guide for the use of the *posttransition* specifier, which is added as an extra name to the gender dysphoria diagnosis, explicitly limits it to a context of continuity in the medical procedures that serve the new gender assignment. In other words, it anchors the diagnosis to clinically transsexualised bodies while they remain subject to the medical protocol, which is virtually for life, as is the prescription of so-called sex hormones and consequent endocrinological monitoring.

This implies, at root, that every person who receives a gender dysphoria diagnosis will retain the diagnosis as long as they continue to be in transit in medical institutions (their entire life, according to the normative prescription of monitoring by medical experts) despite the interventions they are subject to. This contradicts Patricia Soley-Beltrán's conclusion (2013) that in the new manual "the pathology is no longer considered to be permanent as it is considered to disappear potentially after treatment" (p. 50). This is likely to be translated as an institutional recognition of the failure of the scientific promise that considers medical treatment to be the corrector of the *gender incongruence* it diagnoses,[13] a promise of a *congruence* able to open the door to membership of a legitimated gender.

What I have wanted to emphasise here is a rhetorical exercise that – while appearing to free (diagnosed) bodies from clinical interventions (displacements of the requirement of interventions in the diagnostic criteria, for example) – actually develops new strategies to anchor the diagnosis in medical practice, by making the category depend on its transit (or intention to transit) through the *correction* technologies. While transsexuality appears pictured as a distress that depends on (non)access to clinical intervention, and in which the need or desire for such access permeates the guidelines for its diagnosis and even functions as a criterion that differentiates it from other psychiatric diagnoses, it is the same category that remains fixed to its medical protocolarisation, constructed clinically as hospital dependency.

Speaking of treatments, what is being treated?

Let us return to the earlier quotation and continue our analysis, now to visibilise how a psychopathologising discourse is transmitted even when the narrative may not present it explicitly as such:

> A person who is transsexual, if not treated, will be bad their whole life. Of course [. . .] Because a person cannot live, cannot live with something that they don't feel is their own.
>
> *(Psychiatrist, interview)*

Apart from the rhetorical constructions of transsexuality as an identity doubly condemned to treatment or distress, the quotation gives us no specific information about the kind of clinical approach or the type of correction that the transsexual person might desire or need. Its formulation, although isolated intentionally and chosen to illustrate the direction of this argument, appears comfortable and sufficient within a supposedly shared framework of interpretation that requires no specification to what it refers. The text appears to assume that we all know, although in vague or general terms, what is being treated and how.

However, if we read the quotation from the distance allowed us by our suspicion from the beginning of the words and their concrete arrangements of sense (Fairclough, 1989/2001; Santander, 2011), if for a moment we allow ourselves to take distance from the surface of meanings in which the quotation is situated, we can see that the obviousness to which it refers vanishes, or at least becomes ambiguous. Even after our journey through various discursive and clinical constructions about transsexuality, we do not know if the quotation refers to the psychiatric category's homogenising effects on the experiences of life it defines, or whether it refers to a body or its parts as cultural signifiers of membership of one or other of the strict, socially delimited, parcels of gender.

In other words, we know that transsexuality is constructed as an identification category with its determinations of unity and life coherence. We know also that the body appears arbitrarily signified by cultural discourses as belonging to the category of male or female, without ambiguities. I have analysed how distress, as one of the basic nuclei of the clinical diagnosis and the one precisely legitimating medical interventions, is discursively bound to these bodies and identities and linked closely to the possibility of gaining access to the medical care protocols aimed at the subject's gender reassignment. We have also seen how the category's existence appears constructed in dialogue with the possibility of treatments, which recursively constitute (and are constituted by) the clinical diagnosis. However, beyond our knowledge of the medical technologies applied to transsexual persons and their bodies, we do not know what the concrete object of these interventions is, or clearer still, what it is they claim to correct.

At this point I shall attempt an analytical proposal about what appears here to be technologically treatable. Even though palliation of distress is presented as the social legitimation for medical interventions (Coll-Planas, 2010b; Garaizabal, 2010), I shall exclude it from the analysis since, as I have argued earlier, the distress is configured in dependence on experiences associated with the dominant constructions of the body and/or of gender identities. In both cases, whether in combination or separately, distress is common to the possible explanations traceable in psychiatric discourse, which is why I will focus here on the concrete object of clinical intervention, whose ultimate objective is to eliminate a distress that has been instituted discursively and anchored to experiences defined by these elements.

Body and identity are two elements of the psychiatric rhetoric that appear and reappear in the narratives we have reviewed, through a fiction of boundary and communion, but clearly differentiable. An example is the first criterion of DSM-5 for gender dysphoria, defined as we have seen by a marked gender *incongruence* (assigned versus expressed), in which some of the guidelines for the criterion are "A strong desire to be rid of one's primary and/ or secondary sex characteristics *because of* a marked incongruence with one's experienced/expressed gender" or "A strong *desire to be* of the other gender" (APA, 2013, p. 452). This reproduces a dualism between Nature and Culture, Body and Identity, in which one member of the pair must respond to and be congruent with the other, as if they were two pieces of a jigsaw puzzle, both lacking sense without the other, although each constructed quite independently of the other.

The question, then, would be: is what is technologically treatable here what psychiatry understands as transsexual identity? Or does it refer us to the body of the person defined as transsexual?[14]

The (un)finished bodies of psychiatry

At the end of the sentence, where it says "a person cannot live, cannot live with something that they don't feel is their own", it seems obvious that this something refers to the body or parts of it (those parts that are interpreted as signs of membership of one or other of the sexual categories: male or female). It refers us to a mandatory requirement that one appropriate one's own anatomy, that one feel one's body (and each of its parts) as one's own and as desirable in order to be able to live. It implies a mandate of coherence and unity, at the same time as a static gaze in recognition of a body objectified and fragmented.

This conception of the anatomy as of obligatory ownership, directed at someone who must identify with it completely in order to live, implies the determination of a subjectivity that must be coherent not with the corporal image, but with the social meanings that have been constructed and attached to certain parts of the body through the sex/gender system as a regulatory device. It responds to a structural bond between productions of gender identity and of certain organs classified as sexual (Preciado, 2000/2011, 2008/2015) whose maladjustment or non-recognition falls into the territory of the unviable, erroneous and pathological.

Through the destiny the end of this quote imposes ("a person cannot live, cannot live with something that they don't feel is their own"), medicine – the only authorised owner of the technologies needed to manage one's own body – becomes legitimated in exercising authority in the field of gender nonconformities. By reproducing a fictitious frontier and communion between body and subjectivity, reinforced as unquestionable, ahistorical and pre-social as a result of its naturalisation and subjection to biology (Roselló &

Cabruja, 2012), the knowledge-power of psychiatry, which sustains this discursive construction, makes of body modification a "necessity" that is indispensable to make life possible for persons diagnosed as transsexual, who have been subjectivated as inhabitants of bodies that have been expropriated,[15] disadjusted and thus in need of rehabilitation.

Following the reflection of Ezequiel Lozano (2009), if what has a pressing need for technological treatment is the body, we could counterpose the idea that every body is technologically intervened, or rather, correction, every body is a technological and political production (Haraway, 1991; Preciado, 2008). In this specific sentence of treatment, then, are we being told that the bodies of transsexual persons and only theirs are in some way incomplete and subject to processes of rehabilitation? We know that the "terms of gender designation are thus never settled once and for all but are constantly in the process of being remade" (Butler, 2004, p. 10), a process that leads to a continuous reworking of corporal intelligibility, which passes, among other operations, through the use of language and designations of sex (linking supposed anatomies with supposed realities), the prescription and imitation of movements, as well as through more or less daily cosmetic interventions. "Why would all this be necessary if [. . .] the body of the transsexual is the only one that is unfinished?" (Lozano, 2009, p. 7).

Between creation and negation: the unlivable identity of transsexuality

Now, continuing with this wholly fictitious frontier between Nature and Culture, Body and Identity, if it is transsexual identity that must be treated, then it implies a definition of an illegitimate space (Garaizabal, 1998, 2010), and that there are other identities that should be obtained to overcome it. Whatever they are (although we know what they are), transsexuality is constructed as an uninhabitable territory or one that should be disinhabited, as an identity-sentence to either treatment or distress.

To clarify the presence of this discourse, I propose a synthesis exercise. If we eliminate the intervention of medicine in this small fragment of the narration, that is the references to treatment and the consequences of not undergoing it, the paragraph would read thus:

> A person who is transsexual, if not treated, will be bad their whole life. Of course [. . .] Because a person cannot live, cannot live with something that they don't feel is their own.

> (A person who is transsexual cannot live, cannot live with something that they don't feel is their own.)

If discourses do not only describe but also construct reality, what is presented here as a description of an experience of life can be read as a construction of transsexuality as an impossibility of life. It is the reproduction of a dominant discourse that disqualifies certain bodies, those, we are told, that are the inappropriable space of the subjective position created by the medical category "transsexual".

In other words, this sentence could be interpreted as a disciplinary imposition toward life. With another simple effort of synthesis, this time including the allusion to treatment, the statement tells us:

> A person who is transsexual, if not treated, ~~will be bad their whole life.~~ ~~Of course [. . .] Because a person~~ cannot live, ~~cannot live with some=~~ ~~thing that they don't feel is their own.~~

(A person who is transsexual, if not treated, cannot live.)

Treatment would be an emergency for what is constructed as a transsexual identity and not accessing it would not allow life. Transsexuality, then, appears constructed – not understood, or badly understood, but constructed – as a category that subjectifies in death. It is a discourse in which transsexuality is not only delegitimised as a state of passage, a place that is only inhabitable temporarily, but also as a road leading no less than to one's own life. It is constructed not only as a transitory state, but also as a non-existence from which medicine and its interventions must produce an intelligible subject.

I do not speak here of a politics of administration of death, in terms that could imply a thanatopolitics, but of a normative control of life in which the knowledge-power of medicine grants recognition to transsexual experience that does not recognise its status of life. It concerns the construction (the clinical knowledge of transsexuality gives it a whole conceptual framework) of a "living figure outside the norms of life" (Butler, 2009a, p. 8), that must be managed in order to fit within a framework of intelligibility/normativity that can provide it with the conditions that make possible its recognition as life. Legitimate life, recognisable life, livable life.

Expressed differently, for the heterosexual and clinical norm of the healthy to exist as the only truth, it is necessary that there be no legitimate alternatives. But what doubt is there: such possibilities do exist. Although the exception does not make the rule, the latter does make the exception, and it is precisely in this act that we can observe with clarity how the psychiatric ritual is deployed: it individualises what is social-relational and reinterprets as *faulty* what the same discipline has constructed as *disadjustment*, translating it into an unintelligible identity-body duality, outside the gender norms. That is, psychiatry conceptualises the lives it diagnoses but does not recognise their status as life, configuring their bodies and subjective positions as uninhabitable or impossible. The clinic's task will be to achieve this recognition that its own knowledge has denied. How? By showing itself to be a technology for adjusting or readjusting these lives, in order thereby to reveal *the truth*: it constructs an unfinished body, a no-body in order to make it the object of interventions capable of completing it, and makes life illegible in order to decipher it in a legitimate identity.

Notes

1 In 2009, the Stop Trans Pathologization platform (www.stp2012.info) launched its annual call for an international day of action for trans depathologisation. Since then, it takes place every year in October, with coordinated activities in several cities around the world.
2 The definitions are from the Oxford English Dictionary (www.oed.com) and the Royal Academy of the Spanish Language (www.rae.es), respectively.
3 It should be noted that this latter substitution is not replicated in the diagnosis of "Other specified gender dysphoria", which states that "this category applies to presentations in which symptoms characteristic of gender dysphoria *that cause* clinically significant distress or impairment in social, occupational, or other important areas of functioning predominate but do not meet the full criteria for gender dysphoria".
4 This is the definition the Oxford English Dictionary gives for the term distress in its online version: "Extreme anxiety, sorrow, or pain" (www.oed.com).
5 In this regard, the psychoanalyst Patricia Castillo (personal communication, 13 June 2017) points out:

> In this sense, what is rejected and identified in the place of "is me in the mirror" responds, precisely, to the cultural meanings around which the imaginary aspect of the Ego is constituted. To the mirror stage, which recognises the function of the Other in proposing a you are or imposing it on a subject in formation, is attributed the function of organising a body. That "my worst enemy is me in the mirror" is presented as a rejection of the set of libidinal investitures that link a body to a gender, and thereby to expectations of behaviour and future. The clarity with which the schism is manifested between these two parts of the Ego – one which is due to the narcissistic legacy of the Other, and the other that has been created by incorporating that real that remains outside this imaginary organisation – shows a tragic interpellation in which the self-same body is a battlefield between what is most own and what is most alien. A process that implies getting rid of the investitures through which I am or I was an object of the Other's love and care, at the expense of own safety. In that respect, "my worst enemy is me" is a precise and brutal term to describe this process.

6 The difficulties transgender people have in gaining employment and the associated economic precariousness they face have been widely documented. For example, in an investigation carried out with 6,450 transgender people, the

National Center for Transgender Equality and the National Gay and Lesbian Task Force (2009) found that the population studied had double the unemployment rate of the general population; that 97% reported harassment or mistreatment on the job; that 19% of the sample was, or is, homeless; and that 26% lost their jobs for reasons attributable only to their transgender status. A report by the European Network of Legal Experts in the non-discrimination field (2012), stated that "the Engendered Penalties Study shows that only 31% of the participants are in full-time employment [...] Spanish research into unemployment amongst transgender people showed that 54% of the respondents were unemployed" (p. 19).

7   In a similar sense, Raewyn Connell (2010) notes how medically induced body changes are typically associated with transition experiences that are signified as personal projects, neither political nor collective.

8   In the same line, the manual states, "Given the increased openness of atypical gender expressions by individuals across the entire range of the transgender spectrum, it is important that the clinical diagnosis be limited to those individuals whose distress and impairment meet the specified criteria" (p. 458).

9   "In both adolescent and adult natal males, there are two broad trajectories for development of gender dysphoria: early onset and late onset" (APA, 2013, p. 455).

10   The initial battery of psychopathological evaluation usually includes the SCID-II (international examination of personality disorders), ISRA (Inventory of Situations and Responses of Anxiety), Beck Depression Inventory (BDI) and CES-D, Watson's FNE and SAD for the evaluation of Social Phobia, a protocol for suicidal risk and for the evaluation of the consumption of psychoactive substances, a quality of life questionnaire and an evaluation of eating disorders (Berguero & Cano, 2006).

11   "However, individuals with social anxiety disorder often overestimate the negative consequences of social situations, and thus the judgment of being out of proportion is made by the clinician" (APA, 2013, p. 204).

12

> In adolescents and adults, the disturbance is manifested by symptoms such as preoccupation with getting rid of primary and secondary sex characteristics (e.g., request for hormones, surgery, or other procedures to physically alter sexual characteristics to simulate the other sex) or belief that he or she was born the wrong sex. (APA, 1994, p. 538)

13   "Such distress may, however, be mitigated by supportive environments and knowledge that biomedical treatments exist to reduce incongruence" (APA, 2013, p. 455).

14   Apart from a few modifications, the analysis presented in the two following subsections was published in Roselló (2013, pp. 62–64).

15   With the expression "expropriated bodies", I refer to the power effects of the cultural and normative semantic closure of the body or its parts, whose non-recognition is transformed into dichotomous incoherence or the subjective impossibility of bodily appropriation.

CONCLUSION

Writing this book has been an attempt to bring to the surface the polyphony of discourses that reproduce, resist or reconfigure the construction of transsexuality inside the psychological and psychiatric clinic. By disentangling, as it were, the multivocality nearly always present in narratives and their configurations, my aim has been to help clarify the strategies that make transsexuality into an entity outside the limits of intelligibility, one that is organically delimited and medically treatable as a condition that will inevitably lead to suffering. The underlying purpose has been to contribute to the practices of resistance against the violent effects of medico-social constrictions, particularly in their normative constructions of bodies, sexualities and identities.

Critical psychology and discourse analysis have pointed out explicitly that pure or consistent discourses that are without ambiguities or contradictions should be approached with some doubt. Although the dominant discursive orders can be isolated and abstracted, understanding their (often violent) effects requires deciphering the multiplicity of voices with which they participate in subjectifying subjects. Disparities in their narratives, argumentative turns, legitimations that have recourse to one or another discursive genre, negations and obstructions and, above all, the sophisticated mechanisms that articulate them are what give life and body to the texts that constitute us; texts that, no less importantly, we also manage, modify, subvert and (re)create through our social practices and linguistic actions.

On our way here we have seen how flesh goes through a (complex and multiform) series of techno-discursive operations that configure it as a body and a sexed body. The body's sexualised parts are charged with the power to hyper-signify the body as a gendered totality involving a rigorous heteronormative disciplining of their presence/function, to the point of denying or assigning recognition of what is feminine or masculine. A presence and function which also are problematically articulated with erotic desire as a gendered source and destination, all of which configure a field of heterosexual compulsion that acts as a criterion of adjustment and serves as the ultimate determinant in sexual assignment.

Social-cultural recognitions of people, as necessarily sexed beings, are suspended when the coordinates of bodies, genders and desires do not coincide with one another. Through juridico-clinical interdiscursivity, for example, bodies (and their sexual encounters) are pushed toward a normative adjustment, while appearing as impossible, non-textual entities confronted by a continuously renewed process of expulsion. Constructions of *no-bodies* that have violent effects in the lives of those people signified in them. Nonetheless, for those people, these constructions do not univocally determine the articulation of their bodies and sexualities, and are indeed constantly turned back on themselves and re-signified through re-articulations and multiplications of a necessarily unstable interiority.

We saw also how these articulations of bodies and identities are discursively legitimated as products of nature, how the clinic and medical science give them a discursive circulation that is subordinated and colonised by biological hypotheses that in turn are presented as unproblematic and free from the tensions raised by (post)feminist and queer contributions. The biological rhetoric works as a normative and universal imposition of linear evolutionary development that places transsexuality, constructed as an imbalance, within the realm of medicine and its interventions. This discursive construction of the category functions as an organic configuration, surgical and hormonally modifiable, of what is feminine or masculine (through the prescription of chemical-subjective formulae), categories that are organised hierarchically, and understood as expressions of a gender identification that is contained in neuro-molecules.

When this scientific knowledge is articulated with the diagnostic requirements, the construct of gender identity emerges as doubly biologised, as a product of chemical-cerebral factors (biological men and women), or as a biologically determined performative ability. In other words, as a linear organic expression or as an imitation of the other sex (contrary to the assigned one) which is only possible if biology (*victim* of a crossed linear development) permits it, in an operation that at the same time de-naturalises and re-naturalises gender identities in their performative version.

The third chapter explored at length the psychopathologisation of trans-sexuality (the regulatory operation that lies behind the rhetorics of scientific objectification involved in biologisation). I proposed there an organisation of sense of different approaches to this issue, beginning with the identification of distress not just as a symptom tied to the category but fundamentally as the central axis around which transsexuality is constructed as an identity. Firmly anchored in biology, this explanation (which like every other, including the most sociological, implies a communion between the effects of exclusion and the effects of intelligibity on objectivated lives) first de-politicises transsexuality as a heteronormative short-circuit (locating it within an erroneous foetal nature). Then it relocates the consequences of what it has depoliticised – the violent effects of normative social regulations – inside individuals, through a translation into conflictive or suffering identities and emotional states.

This productive feature of the *disorder* (of identity and suffering, or better said, of identity-suffering) appears constructed as a source of problems in the milieu the subject inhabits, or as a source of distress within and by the sub-ject. It works by converting the body into a frontier dividing an inner and an outer world, in possible communication but also in total isolation. It acts by disavowing the relational field in which the world as well as subjectivities and corporalities are constituted and constrained, hampering the emergence of discourses in which social meanings and socially structuring power relations are what provide sense to the distress that persons labelled as transsexual can experience.

This distress, which originates supposedly in the embodied experience of a clinically defined category, has a dual role in psychiatric operations: on the one hand, it is an effect, a product of transsexuality; on the other, it is a cause, a generator of the psychiatric category. In other words, the person suffers because they *have* gender dysphoria, yet it is only possible to say they *have it* because they suffer. It is a circular, tautological discourse, but once constituted is capable of attributing even a third role to distress, possibly the most relevant of all: it makes its presence not only a diagnostic necessity but also a factor sufficient in itself to confirm the urgency of the person's medical treatment. Subjects as patients, constructed as containers of a suffering challenged by the psychological sciences, which legitimate their own interventions by pre-senting themselves as committed to freeing the subject from everything that, paradoxically, subjects them, wagering on an individual(ised) wellbeing, one that is implicated in the very idea of mental health.

The subject also appears dually constructed. On the one hand, the subject is configured as a passive recipient of the distress determined by a body-subjectivity in conflict (passive because the subject does not manage or preside over this conflict, but suffers from it by being also the biological receptacle of a disorder).Yet, on the other hand, the subject is constructed as responsible for their desire and for the predicament of incorporating this hyper-signified and desocialised body. In this exercise of individualisation and psychologisation of oppressions, mediated by a confession ritual in which social-relational experiences are converted into a symptomatology and the subject into an object of clinical appraisal, mental health is placed under suspicion and other psychiatric categories emerge as liable to being co-diagnosed, such as social phobia. In this exercise, the *psy sciences* – scientific bastions of the neoliberal contraband of wellbeing and individual freedom – are unveiled as prescribers of good and bad mental health, producing and regulating subjects, their behaviours and their ways of being in the world according to their clinical maxims – discourses which at the same time normalise the social violences they reproduce while exonerating the latter of responsibility for their effects.

The subjects defined by the clinical category are anchored to the medical treatments that recursively categorise them, while the latter present themselves as the route that must be followed for the subjects to be removed from the psychiatric catalogues (but only relatively so, ever since the inclusion of a post-transition specifier in the most recent edition of the DSM). Here, the discourse analysis carried out called into question the object of these medical interventions, through an artificial dichotomisation exercise that, nonetheless, attempted to reproduce the dualisms belonging to the studied discourses. By asking if it is the body or identities that are configured as being technologically intervenable, we saw how both dimensions are constructed as pathological and in need of clinical operations.While the body is configured as incomplete, incoherent and thereby undesirable, the identity of people diagnosed as transsexuals appears as an uninhabitable land, as a non-identity invaded by a suffering associated with this specific body's signification. By means of the discursive analysis of a small fragment, we found a possible response for the medical urgency of dual treatments: a disciplinary imposition toward life, mediated by a subjectification of the subjects-objects of intervention as moribund people.

Having reached this point, I find it necessary to finalise this book by exploring in greater depth, as an epilogue, the discursive construction of transsexual persons as unintelligible (or what I shall refer to here as monstrogenesis), and about the effects of what I propose as their resultant subjectification in death. What follows is a review of some related theoretical contributions, which are problematised through the conceptualisation of homo/transphobia and some tragic examples of its various forms of violence.

MONSTROGENESIS AND MONSTROLYSIS

The regulative production of death (epilogue)

In Ricardo Llamas's view (1998), homosexuality, as an abstraction situated outside the limits of legitimate life, must have been constructed in opposition to the heterosexual ideals (and recognised rights) of the pursuit of happiness and wellbeing. Hence homosexuality's close connection with suffering as an intrinsic aspect of its experience and, consequently, with suicide as both a predestined path and a confirmation that these are lives not worth living. Moreover, they would be subjects of death because they have been consti- tuted as incapable of procreation, implying disdain for their own and other lives, due either to the imaginary of an incapability of establishing and main- taining meaningful affective relationships, or to the existential or vital empti- ness associated with "bulimic" sexual practices. All this was reinforced by the AIDS pandemic in the 1980s, which anchored to their bodies a humiliating and premature death, one that was, above all, sought after, deserved or rather always carried within them.

Judith Butler agrees in pointing out that the homosexual's body has been consistently represented in terms of the desire to die, or of acting out a desire that is itself a death sentence (Butler, 1992). The ever-present possibility of death relates to an understanding of the norm as a requirement of life, so that placing oneself outside it is the same as not desiring life, or directly looking for death. Assassination, then, is a "vain and violent effort to restore order, to renew the social world on the basis of intelligible gender" (Butler, 2004, p. 34).

I agree with both approaches toward the bodies of otherness. However, in this epilogue I want to focus on a point that while not foreign to both authors (especially to Judith Butler) highlights another aspect of the power operations that subjectify these bodies. I argue that these bodies are acted upon by a disciplinary imposition toward life (acting upon bodies, no doubt, but with regulatory objectives), which is reinforced, not questioned, by the idea that homosexual and transsexual bodies serve as containers of death or are even death itself. However, I maintain that, leaving aside the case of murder, to which I will return later, the function of that most classic of devices regulating the heterosexual norm, the insult – or what is similar but not equal to it, the *world of insults* (Eribon, 1999/2004) – is not to inscribe these bodies with death, inferiority or anomaly in relation to a hierarchically constructed social order, even though, of course, the insult does this too. Rather, its function is to re-actualise the norm by constituting its "opposite" (on the basis of which it is constructed) as threatened by punishment. The purpose of this re-actualisation through the insult, or in this case through pathologisation and the discourses that sustain it, is that the subject be absorbed by the norm; that is, the reactualisation of the norm is not satisfied with the mere construction of the subject as an opposite.

Insults embarrass, humiliate and turn given lives and their experiences into errors; as such, theirs is a violent invitation for concealment or for "correction". This is not to deny that in a world of insults, death literally is present as a possibility, if not as an objective. But, even if death is not its real aim from a physical point of view, the importance of the insult as a phenomenon is its production of certain bodies as insultable. The insult installs the truth of the unintelligibility *of* the body *on* the body to which it is aimed, constituting it as *a non-existent existence*. Simply put, it tells us which bodies should not exist, or indeed which bodies have never existed, precisely because insult is the performative production of these bodies, but it does so in order to proclaim how one must live.

Homo/transphobia: an architecture of collapse

Perhaps one of the most potent and visible mechanisms by which the construct of gender and its heterosexual foundation regulate the population is what we know as homophobia (also known as anti-gay/lesbian hate), and transphobia. If we approach their forms of violence conceptually as acts of insult, we could say, along with Didier Eribon (2000), that they are "the expression of asymmetry between individuals, between those who are legitimate and those who are not, and for the same reason, are vulnerable" (p. 55). It operates *as* a discourse of domination by some over others (with concrete effects, doubtless, on the lives involved), but is a regulatory device that involves each and every subjectivity. Some are the insultable subjects who have been objectified by insult; others, constructed in reference to the expelled model, and thus interpellated by the selfsame possibility of insult. In any case, lives worth living are on one side, and lives that are non-gratifying, precarious or just impossible are on the other (Butler, 2009a, 2009b).

In his critical reading of Daniel Borillo, Gerard Coll-Planas (2010a) writes:

> [Homo/transphobia] plays the role of a "sexuality police", repressing any behaviour, gesture or desire that overruns the borders of gender [. . .] the cause of the aversion to gays and lesbians is that by breaking with the norm of man/woman complementarity in their choice of object, they alter the rules of gender [. . .] For this reason we consider that transphobia (vigilance over sex/gender correspondence) is at the root of homophobia, that it regulates an aspect of it.
>
> *(p. 101)*

I agree that the "sexuality police" (Borillo, 2001, p. 95), "cultural heteronormative police" (Bersani, cited in Eribon, 2000, p. 40) or the "gender police" (Gordo, 1995, p. 133) are the effect of and reason for homo/transphobia, and hence the focus of the insult is on the regulation of "sex" insofar as gender and heterosexual regime. So I also coincide in considering transphobia or "vigilance of the sex/gender correspondence" as a regulatory device of bodies involved in sexual activity, at the root of homophobia, where both tactics of oppression (homophobia and transphobia) "form part of the same phenomenon, but have different causes, intensities and forms of expression" (Coll-Planas, 2010a, p. 101).

However, this definition makes use of the concepts in a way I consider problematic. This is perhaps more explicit in the following excerpt:

> We use homophobia to refer to the oppression received by persons who choose a homosexual object, and transphobia to that suffered by trans people, but more generically by all men and women when they depart from the normative expression of gender.
>
> *(Coll-Planas, 2010a, p. 102)*

If, as I have been arguing, the device of sexuality constitutes these bodies as no-bodies and their respective sexualities as unrecognisable, then homophobia is not limited to an oppression (received or suffered) that is due to the choice of a homosexual object. This is because it does not work by punishing the orientation of desire, but by making it recognisable as unrecognisable. This was made perhaps most patently obvious with the emergence of the

AIDS epidemic, when those who had lost their partners to AIDS found it impossible to explain or gain recognition for their mourning, given that, from the beginning, subjects and their emotional relationships were *nothing* (Butler, 2009b).

If oppression were directed at *sexual orientation*, it would mean that there was something there (the source and an object of a gendered desire), that the desiring bodies would be recognised. On the contrary, we become possible as people in terms of our reading in and by the heterosexual matrix, in which desire appears constructed at the intersection of genders between intelligible corporal-sexual unities, a question I addressed in the first chapter. So, conceptually speaking, punishment is not aimed at the homosexual desire because this desire, being a precondition, has not had the possibility of constituting itself as recognisable. Oppression works, then, by making this desire impossible, by configuring it as monstrous due to its constitution (in the image of intercourse and pleasures) as an incorrect prosthetic assemblage of body parts, incoherent in their presence and functionality, un-nameable, non-sexual flesh incapable of carrying out any practice that could be deemed sexual.

This is not to say, of course, that the violence experienced by persons with homoerotic practices bears no relation to their sexual objects, placed on stage through affective practices and relations. Homosexual persons (not homosexuality) have been made recognisable insofar as what is denied about them are signs that are not necessarily visible. Recognition is acquired by silencing what is not recognisable (Mira, 2004; Borillo, 2001), as a "right to the *visible invisibility*" (Bourdieu, 1998/2001, p. 121). What I want to convey, then, is that the norm functions by constituting or denying recognition of persons and desires as being legitimate, rather than acting on or against *something* that it does not conceptualise as existing. Or better said, something that it constructs in a limbo, half phantasmic, half real. In other words, the norm actualises itself by (re)formulating itself and insult forms part of that formulation; yet, the level at which it operates is not that of punishing desire, but of actualising and recreating its monstrousness, as something inapprehensible due to its non-existence according to the (hetero)normative codes.

In similar fashion, "men and "women" do not suffer transphobia when they depart from the normative expression of gender. Fundamentally, this is because gender norms are precisely what turn bodies into men and women; it is in this field that their oppressive forces are in play, in which the lack of normative correspondence deforms bodies into a state of unrecognisability/ monstrosity. Gender norms are what constitute *people*, recognisable or not, and the oppression involved in transphobia is the actualisation of the same productive norm, in the normative sense, not a question of it being applied as a law. The construction of transsexuality as a monstrosity is in itself the transphobic effect of the norm.

The medical discourse and its diagnostic and intervention technologies, then – together with the construction of the category of transsexual as an amalgam of discontinuous body parts, as a boundary object (Gordo, 1995) where, in accessing intelligibility, recognition intersects with denial – work as a machinery of monstrogenesis. Their expert apprehension reinforces the social construction of monstrousness, in which the definitions of correct bodies, functions and pleasures situate persons diagnosed as transsexual in a limbo between what is possible and what is not, and in this mixture they are disarticulated as a possible existence. In the best case, it situates these people as a textualisation project through pathological construction and its therapeutic resolution.

Homo and *trans* bodies are not outside the norm; in fact, they are the most finished product of the norm. This is precisely because the norm limits their entelechy to what is not – entirely – possible, given their non-ideal constitution when compared to a fiction of masculinity and femininity that actually no one fully embodies or is able to fully embody. These bodies are insulted, raped, beaten, killed and disappeared, precisely because insult, rape, beatings, death and disappearance form part of their construction, in a way that bears similarities to (but is not the same as) the way in which collapse is a possibility that is built into the architecture of any building. The difference here is that, in this case, we are dealing specifically with an architecture of collapse, or rather – so as not to lose the thread of our argument due to the language being used – with an architecture of the non-existent. As a monstrous limbo, the category's component elements provide it with a two-way street between disappearance and emergence, both of which are contained within the transsexual corporality and complement one another in the disciplinary imposition toward life, which is governed by medical protocols that are tied for a lifetime to the transsexual person's constitution as a subject.

Regardless of their particularities and the political and legal needs to increase their visibility, what we refer to as transphobia and homophobia should be read as performative repetitions of the norm as it constructs bodies as impossibles. I propose the term *monstrolysis* to conceptualise the process that underlies homophobic and transphobic aggression (not as a substitute for those concepts), where the adjunct *lysis* is understood as dissolution, decomposition or disintegration. Dissolution, decomposition or disintegration of the monstrous, as a process that constitutes it normatively, in that it involves the construction of bodies, sexualities and subjectivities that contain non-existence within themselves. Based on this dialectic between monstrogenesis and monstrolysis, these *lives that do not matter* are constituted as containers for both death and life. Here, the possibility of life depends on the construction of its ever actualised opposite. Furthermore, life is only ever possible in a precarious way, immersed as it is in a never-ending corporal-subjective battle for intelligibility that hinges on escaping the decomposition/dissolution offered by medicine, the same medicine that collaborates in the social construction of monstrosity.

As Didier Eribon (1999/2004) points out, insult (or we could say homophobic and transphobic insult) is a performative statement: "Insult tells me what I am to the extent that it makes me be what I am" (p. 17). Through insult, bodies are subjectified, created and moulded. What I am suggesting is to take this performativity of insult to its extreme, not only to show that its enunciation (or realisation in a physical action) is constitutive of being, that it is "expression (and construction) of the asymmetry of individuals" (Eribon, 2000, p. 55), but rather to show how the selfsame aggressions *are* the monstrosity, its performative repetitions of itself. Hence, homophobia and transphobia can be conceptualised as attributes of a sort of monstrolysis or dissoluble-monstrosity/decomposing-monstrosity; rather than acting upon monstrous bodies, they themselves are those monstrous bodies. They do not recall them, reinforce them, mark them or actualise them – they are part of the very constitution of monstrosity as a material, machinery, labour force and product of the architecture of the non-existent.

Death as an operation, life as an objective

When Michel Foucault (1976/1978) establishes sex as a cornerstone of productive power, tracing its development back to the progression from the eighteenth to the nineteenth century, he refers us to a gradual retreat, although not without overlaps, of sovereign, coercive or juridical power, where blood was the fundamental element of power mechanisms whose management centred on death. Judith Butler's critical reading relativises this overcoming of the disciplinary power by a regulatory one, taking the overlap to the extreme by showing that juridical power has always been productive power:

> What this suggests, of course, is that there is no historical shift from juridical to productive power but that juridical power is a kind of dissimulated or concealed productive power from the start and that the shift, the inversion, is within power, not between two historically or logically distinct forms of power.
>
> *(Butler, 1992, pp. 349–350)*

In other words, death would never have been "the term, the limit, or the end of power", as Foucault argued (1976/2003, p. 248). The production of the category of sex, its exclusionary and unified ascription through identity, which is the category's most coercive operation, is marked by mortality. I refer not only to sex as sexuality and specifically to semen as carrier of both life and of death too in the post-AIDS era (something that, as Butler and Llamas point out, Foucault could not have foreseen), but also to sex as an identity, produced through the configuration of the non-existent. Power not only circulates administering and producing life, guaranteeing the viability and legitimacy of reproductive bodies, because the very exercise of power implies a specific normative construction of what life is, and by extension, what it is not:

> This is not a shift from a version of power as constraint or restriction to a version of power as productive but a production that is *at the same time* constraint, a constraining in advance of what will and will not qualify as a properly sexed being.
>
> *(Butler, 1992, p. 350)*

At this point I would dissent from, or rather question, a specific assertion of Judith Butler when she says, "One ought not to think that by saying yes to power, one says no to death, for death can be not the limit of power but *its very aim*" (1992, p. 360, emphasis added). I would argue instead that although death has never ceased being regulated and has always been produced, the ultimate aim of power is the production (of certain forms) of life; here, death does not constitute a destiny (as Butler holds) but is a constitutive and necessary part of managing life. Death is produced in order to produce life, managing bodies via their possibility of correction or survival through the same operations that have constituted it as non-life or as dead-life, while cloaking this exercise and feigning the existence of an objective body that is simply described by a coercive power. As Foucault points out (1976/1978), referring to wars and genocide, killing is "waged on behalf of the existence of everyone [. . .] power is situated and exercised at the level of life" (p. 137). Yet – and here I differ – death is not "power's limit, the moment that escapes it" (p. 138), but rather a fundamental operation (not an objective) of the same regulatory power that seeks to optimise life.

Death is not what is excluded from the production of life because the very same production of forms of life necessarily implies the production of what is not life. But I suggest that production itself should not be confused with production as an objective. That something is necessarily produced when, however disguised, the attempt is made to produce its opposite, does not imply that power operates at the level of death, but rather it is the level of death that is produced at the level of life. Despite the fact that death is carefully controlled and life is guaranteed through this production and regulation, it is at the level of life that power both operates and is inexhaustible. Power's purpose, constantly actualised, is to produce life, to construct what is controllable and can be regulated and optimised, a purpose that is achieved by producing what does not exist, or if it does exist, is not readable; or, if it is readable it is only readable through the codes of legitimacy that do not recognise it. The purpose is achieved, then, as long as the ceaseless production of death is guaranteed, or, what is the same thing, life is produced under the necessary condition of death.

Perhaps this is clearer in the explanation that Foucault gives of the superimposition of these technologies of power, both of which are technologies of the body: on the one hand as an individualised body, and on the other as bodies that are relocated through biological processes of the collective social body. Given that both mechanisms, or sets of mechanisms, are not on the same level, they are not exclusive of one another but in most cases, one is articulated over the other. It is precisely at this technological intersection that sexuality is to be found, a realm of both discipline (in its most corporal form) and of regulation (in its biological-populational extension via its procreative consequences). And in the midst of this articulation between the body and the biological multiplicity, we encounter the norm and the society of normalisation (Foucault, 1976/2003).

We are left, then, with the social normalisation of sexuality as the cornerstone in the articulation of these two technologies of the body, and a power capable of generating not only desirable life, but also life that is undesirable and monstrous. And, being monstrous, contaminating, dangerous for the biological safety of the whole. And just as racism operates as a biological-type relationship, as

> the break between what must live and what must die [. . .], the death of the other, the death of the bad race, of the inferior race (or the degenerate or the abnormal) is something that will make life in general healthier: healthier and purer.
>
> *(Foucault, 1976/2003, pp. 254–255)*[1]

This is where, precisely, it becomes possible for the old sovereign power to work through biopower, or for death to be manageable and produced by a technology that regulates and optimises life. The paradox now resolved, death remains more subject to a disciplinary process of regulation than to an objective.

Death as an objective, and more concretely, physical death, can potentially bring to light the existence of determined forms of life and their lack of recognition. In other words, it implies a renunciation of biopower at the same time as the return of sovereign power. Even suicide, which Ricardo Llamas (1998) holds to be normative proof that the life in question was not legitimately a life (or not a desirable life), is susceptible to resignifications that pervert its a priori meaning, calling into question the norm as the only truth (Spivak, 1999). But above all, it is death as an act upon an other that brings to light the violence and artificiality of the norm, making it impossible deny that there was "something" there. As Judith Butler notes,

> When those frames that govern the relative and differential recognisability of lives come apart – as part of the very mechanism of their circulation – it becomes possible to apprehend something about what or who is living but has not been generally "recognized" as a life.
>
> *(2009a, p. 12)*

This is precisely where the gravity of legal impunity and the lack of recognition for a murder committed lies, in that the disappeared (living?) body is denied recognition as a speaking body, as a true body and as a body that destabilises the oppressive norm that has constructed it by silencing it. Death as an objective, in other words, reconstitutes the social order, but does so at the price of relativising this order, of reconstituting it, at every step, in its fictional existence.

Let us consider the legal effects that the most violent acts against marginalised bodies have had in some social contexts. To take a case that is geographically close – it happened in Santiago de Chile, my city of origin – I will refer to the torture and murder of a homosexual young man, Daniel Zamudio. On 3 March 2012, four youths brutally assaulted him after he confessed to them that he was "homosexual", as one of those convicted of the crime later declared. They kicked him until he was unconscious; broke a bottle on his head and, once broken, carved three swastikas with it on his body; burned him with cigarettes; urinated on him; and broke one of his legs. Daniel was left in a coma from which he never recovered; he died 24 days later from the torture.

As a result of the social and media impact of the case, probably because of its graphic link with Nazi symbols – unjustifiable to any "decent" conscience – the State found itself under pressure to approve an antidiscrimination law that recognised "sexual orientation" and "gender identity" as reasons for discrimination, a law mired for years in Congress precisely because of the inclusion of those "problematic" points. Faced by public pressure, and specifically from gay political organisations with legal objectives, the Chilean state and its judicial apparatus were forced to recognise (via the figure of a specific crime) the illegitimacy of the violence against these bodies. It was violence, torture and annihilation, then, that shed light on the existence of the body of otherness, one that was historically denied by the institutional apparatuses that are key to the social recognition of bodies.

By citing the preceding example, I am not claiming that homosexual people in Chile have finally conquered a right that "in its real effects, is much more linked with attitudes and patterns of behaviour, than to legal formulations" (Foucault, 1979/1994, p. 308). What I want to stress with this dramatic case is that the concrete body, the tortured and murdered body, gained access to recognition as alive and liveable *despite* his declaration of being homosexual, but above all, *in* that declaration. The body was dissociated from the death that, nevertheless, it was subjected to under a legal apparatus that until then did not recognise its social construction as killable, and given the same (lack of) legality left unprotected (left to die) in the specificity of its abjection. The body of otherness emerged as possible.

One could argue against this reflection by citing the countless murders suffered by transsexual and homosexual persons that have gone unpunished the world over.[2] To cite another example, since 2013 videos of a civilian collective in Russia called "Occupy Pedofilyaj" have circulated on social networks. Basing themselves on the traditional association and condemnation of a link between homosexuality and paedophilia, these videos contain brutal images of interrogations, humiliations and beatings of homosexual young people and adolescents.[3] Human rights websites denounced the death of one of the homosexual adolescents as a result of the violence suffered, as well as the complicity of the authorities, who claimed to see "any wrongdoings in the video clips or photographs posted by Neo Nazi group 'Occupy Pedofilyaj'. Actually, the authorities referred to this group as one of the 'civil movements fighting the sins of the society'" (Spectrum Human Rights Alliance, 07/08/2013). According to human right groups, all the above is backed by a change in the law promoted by Russian president Vladimir Putin during June of the same year (unanimously approved by the Chamber of Deputies and supported by 88% of the population), which criminalises propaganda of "non-traditional sexual relations" (Human Rights Watch, 06/11/2013).[4]

Examples like these occur every day. The silencing of bodies murdered for reasons of "sexual orientation" or "gender identity" is the rule. Lives that do not matter as lives, carriers of death and unable to speak from their position of illegitimacy. Without denying this, and in agreement with Butler's reading of the device of sexuality as a producer of death, not just of life, I consider that these are coercive operations whose ultimate objective is to produce specific forms of life, through the certainty that death is a possibility whenever something is made visible that does not match the heteronormative standard. Whether or not the murdered body is converted into a text will depend on other factors that give it context, as is the case of the association with Nazism inscribed on the body of the young man murdered in Chile, as well as a legal environment that does not legitimate its inscription. Even so, the death always reveals the existence of "something" behind it, together with the possibility (however uncertain) of a text that subverts, by resignifying, the normative reading that constituted it as non-existent or not-possible.

Even the promulgation of the Russian law, also known as the law against homosexual propaganda, acts as the producer of a certain form of life by establishing a dialogue between the norm and the law. While it does not make explicit which sexual relations are "non-traditional", the law does produce them as antagonists to sexual relations that it constructs as traditional. Within the same text, power relations merge in coercion and production through sex, despite the fact that it appears to merely delimit a sexuality that was already there, as condemnable. In effect, what is hidden is the law's collaboration in the production of "traditional" sexualities, producing sexual practices that are taken to be outside the norm (which in reality contains them). A norm that is founded on tradition and religious beliefs, as this same law was followed by an amendment to the criminal code that "establishes penalties for attacking the sentiments of believers" (Colás, 30/06/2013).

Insofar as a norm that is turned into a law, or an objective that is recoded to take the form of a law, this proposes an optimisation of life according to the Christian canon of what constitutes a "good life", as well as through the protection of children or the rhetoric of the "Child" (Edelman, 2004), to whom this propaganda should not reach – a protection that is in dialogue with the homologation of homosexuality and paedophilia, the same one on which the neo-Nazi group justifies their attacks disseminated on social media. And, at the same time it collaborates in a relational network of power for which the achievement of its objectives also involves "the right to *take* life or *let* live" (Foucault, 1976/1978, p. 136) depending on the ascription or revelation of a "non-traditional" sexuality. This, because its authorities legitimise protagonists of these attacks as combatants against "the sins of society" and imprison and persecute those who "publicise" homosexuality and stand up for their rights (Spectrum Human Rights Alliance, 7/08/2013).[5]

The world of insults, of which murders, torture and laws like the one just referred to are part – as well as the clinical discourses of pathologisation, to return to the topic that concerns us here – and which constructs certain lives as vulnerable, unlawful and anomalous, has the production of legitimate lives as its ultimate objective, its reason. This world of insults forms part of the very construction of what is legitimate through the construction of positions of exteriority, despite the fact that, at the end, are only these last ones that stand out on the surface. "Nothing is more interior to our society, nothing is more interior to the effects of its power than the disgrace of a mad person or the violence of a criminal. In other words, we are always on the interior. Marginality is a myth" (Foucault, 1977/1994, p. 77); the illusion of expulsion is a production that makes possible the delimitation of power's objective: interiority, the norm, the desirable optimised.

Perhaps modern discourses of pathologisation best exemplify the coercive, but above all productive character of power. The main effect of the possibility of a "cure", of a correction, is both to deny the existence of that which has been constructed as exterior to healthfulness, as well as to naturalise and legitimise the interiority that the selfsame discourse produces. In the specific case of transsexuality, pathologisation renders it an unintelligible exterior according to gender norms, necessarily an error faced by the *confirmed* truth of biology. The construction of the fiction *that nothing is possible beyond what is possible*, of a non-life, in reality is a production of specific forms of life as the only ones that are liveable, as the de-pathologising turn in psychology has insistently stressed (Cabruja, 2013). It conceals the fact that at the heart of this productive activity, the exteriority is generated as a necessary part of affirming one sole truth, but this exteriority is illusorily presented as the confirmation of an error that is prior to the norm that actually has configured it as an error.

If the objective of constructing exteriority, or error, were *simply* to eliminate it (as in fact occurs with other technologies of death involved in the sphere of the insult), then interiority would be only fragilely sustainable by the concealment and silencing of bodies that have been subjectified as moribund. In other words, error would have a textual possibility and would be able to access what is real as difference. What I maintain, by contrast, is that these bodies have never been textual but rather have been constituted as a monstrous version or disfigurement of a non-existent original. The error here is susceptible to correction precisely because it is an erroneous manifestation of the original, and it is through this operation that the norm achieves its greatest success: in being revealed, it is confirmed.

The effect of medical treatments meant to correct transsexual bodies, constructed as monstrous, is to reaffirm the norm of the uniqueness of the sexes and their coherence with the hierarchies and systems of oppression that make bodies intelligible. Transsexual people are submitted to this machinery that subjectifies in death or non-existence not to annihilate them (although that in fact occurs) but to make them into the greatest proof of the veracity of the heterosexual norm. A specific management of life as access to the norm, an access imposed under the coercion of insult, pathologisation and the permanent possibility of death.

My purpose in saying this is not to argue in favour of a return of sovereign power in the present power regimes, because I maintain that its objective is the regulation and optimisation of life. Nor do I deny the historical transition that Foucault develops, and Butler questions to some degree through the case of HIV virus and its onslaught on life, which doubtless the philosopher and historian was unable to include in his analysis despite being one of its first ambassadors. I argue, rather, that the management of death works as a disciplinary imposition toward life insofar as it is the very production of the sexual device, playing a central role in the regulation of the population through the dual watershed of both blood and sex, law and norm.

Murder is a constant and certain threat for transsexual persons in different parts of the world; in itself it is the possibility that constitutes transsexuality or monstrolysis. For its part, pathologisation has the dual effect of a disciplinary correction with regulatory objectives, and of ostracism or exclusion from representable life; as normative adequacy is required to access life and is also at the roots of the coercion and disappearance of certain bodies. By appropriating and perverting some Foucauldian concepts, it could be said that this is a disciplining of the body (anatomo-politics) via the subject's subjectification in death with the threat of punishment or disappearance, but for which the goal is the regulation of the population (biopolitics); an anatomo-politics that takes on a sovereign form with a regulatory nature.

The psychopathologisation of transsexuality as a border operation between death and life

When Foucault describes the main features of juridical-discursive power, discussing the "cycle of prohibition", he tells us that power's objective is that "sex renounce itself" under "the threat of a punishment that is nothing other than the suppression of sex. Renounce yourself or suffer the penalty of being suppressed; *do not appear* if you do not want to disappear" (Foucault, 1976/1978, p. 84, emphasis added). Perhaps this is one of the major points of support to make visible how, in the case of the pathologisation of transsexuality, power has not abandoned its sovereign forms of action, for this is exactly the threat to which transsexualised persons find themselves exposed when they "appear". As Judith Butler points out, "*any social displays* of nonidentity, discontinuity, or sexual incoherence will be *punished*, controlled, ostracized, *reformed*" (1992, p. 350, emphasis added).

Medical treatments aimed at the body take on the precise form of this concealment, this not making "social displays" under penalty of "punishment" to be "reformed". As processes of insult (performative constructions of monstrosity), in them is rooted the greatest potential of the transsexual persons' double subjectification in death: their recognition as an unrecognisable that, moreover, must be concealed. If this does not occur, possible ways of silencing them emerge, ways that are the effects of their social construction as a non-life and therefore leave them vulnerable until death (which is nothing more than monstrolysis put into action, a position that is inevitable by reason of its being constitutive). By resisting exposure of the unrecognisable, the subject's recognition as a subject is suspended and displaced to a journey (through the shadows) that will make it possible for them to enter the framework of intelligibility.

The path suggested through this subjectification, at once denoted and transmitted by insult (of which pathologisation itself is part) is none other than an escape route. That is, forswearing being a monster, detaching oneself from transsexuality or, more clearly still, from each and every one of the possibilities of recognition of the unrecognisable body, all of this under the threatening possibility that the conceptual frameworks that define one as unintelligible not only conceal and silence through their symbolic effects, but also lead to the very act of the body's material annihilation.

At this point, a logical and predictable question is why and how what I have called the "architecture of the non-existent" can be presented as a foundation of existence itself. The answer lies in part in what I have already addressed in this book: the construction of a single truth regarding sex-gender-desire,[6] in which all that is "other" does not exist (with the effect that it ought not to exist) and the scientifically legitimated certainty that this is an unquestionable biological fact. But even with this construction of a pre-discursive truth that is without ambiguities and undeniable, we do not know why or how the construction of non-existence leads precisely to its opposite, not without referring to the ultimate scientific effect of this construction: psychopathologisation.

If we understand psychopathologisation to be one dimension of the world of insults in which transsexuality is subjectified (not only transsexual persons, as this concerns a subjectification of the experience of generic non-correspondence, a phenomenon that can be represented even without the physical presence of a subject to be interpellated and, at the same time through which we are all interpellated), the architecture of its non-existence is produced (also) through its conceptualisation as an illness, as an imbalance in healthfulness – healthfulness that the subject can primarily access through the practice of medicalisation.

Insofar as a construction process of the non-existent, or of what does not exist as such, pathologisation functions like monstrogenesis, opening up a two-sided watershed between life and non-existence. Returning to the assertion made by Sedgwick (1990) and problematised in this book this leads the way to genocide or monstrolysis, while at once giving it the recognition that allows it to access intelligibility. Like an infant who is born dead, it occupies a border zone between what is apprehensible as life and what has no possible reading. Nonetheless, its birth is a possible act given that it is contained in a language that only permits the conceptualisation of its emergence as life-not-alive. In similar fashion, although with life as its objective, the construction of transsexuality walks this same tightrope, with the permanent possibility of the abyss as its destination, all the while sustained by the medical protocols that compel it to carry out this balancing act and that, simultaneously, hold out the promise of the rescue platform as a final destination.

In other words, pathologisation turns the non-existence constituted by the norms of intelligibility (which pathologisation is both constitutive of and indebted to) into something that is correctable. And further still, through its language of survival (Bauman, 1992), founded on both the maxims of health and on the Hippocratic Oath in favor of *life*, pathologisation makes this correction a medical imperative and, at the same time, turns this correction into a necessity for the pathologised subject in their desperate pursuit to be recognised and to reach a horizon that promises life. To be or not to be, to remain in the shadows, or rise to the surface resuscitated. A whole dialectic between death and life.

Notes

1 It should be remembered that among the effects of the Nazi persecution and extermination, regarding both the gay and the Jewish genocide (among others), were the silencing, denying or concealment of sexual/affective practices and racial belongings under threat of disappearance and torture. And that in the specific case of the still muted "homosexual holocaust", which also responded to racial objectives (Borillo, 2001), deportations and confinements were marked by attempts to correct homosexual bodies in order "to reintegrate them into the national community" (Tamagne, 2000/2006, p. 424), through "treatments" such as electro-shock, hormonation and castration.

2 Unpunished murders of homosexuals and transsexuals – such as activist Hande Kader (23 years old, Turkey), disappeared and found with her body mutilated and incinerated; nursing student Yeimi Andrea Sommer (26, Chile), insulted, burned and stabbed by neighbours; or sex worker Paola Buen Rostro (25 years old, Mexico), whose murderer, arrested with the gun still in his hand and released for alleged lack of evidence – are the rule. As an example of this, a report by the foundation Colombia Diversa (2015) denounces that all murders of transgender people in Colombia in 2015 (33) have remained unpunished.

3 One of the tools used to "hunt" their victims are mobile phone applications designed for men to contact other men, such as Grindr. According to communications from Grindr to its users in Egypt, the police in that country use the same technique:

> Interact with security. Egypt is arresting LGBT people and cops could be undercover as LGBT to catch you. Please be careful when arranging appointments with people you do not know and take precautions when posting any information that might reveal your identity.

4 Law promoted by the same political party, A Just Russia, which in January 2017 propelled the reform that pulls macho violence out of the criminal sphere and turns it into an administrative fault. The argument, advanced by Senator Elena Mizulina, is precisely to protect the traditional family, which could be threatened if the husband ends up in jail.

   The years following this legislative change have seen a systematic increase in homo/transphobic attacks and harassment. In April 2017, newspapers around the world denounced the unthinkable: the existence of detention and torture centres for homosexuals in Chechnya. This is no longer a question of groups of people covered by the government in their acts of aggression, but of harassment, torture and murder carried out by the state apparatuses themselves. The international denunciation showed the relation between impunity and the denial of the missing lives, when the spokesman of the government of Ramzan Kadyrov – who in 2004 was decorated by President Vladimir Putin with the highest honorary title of the Russian Federation – Alvi Karimov, stated: "you cannot arrest or repress people who just don't exist in the Republic" (Taylor, 09/04/2017).

5 Coercion that also affected the Russian opposition newspaper *Nóvaya Gazeta*, whose report was the first to denounce the existence of illegal detention centres for homosexuals in Chechnya and its barbarism. The information minister even asked the newspaper to publicly apologise for suggesting that there were gay people in Chechnya (Colás, 18/04/2017), while activist Kheda Saratova – a member of the Kadyrov Human Rights Council – pointed out that "any person who respects our traditions and culture will hunt down this kind of person without any help from authorities, and do everything to make sure that this kind of person does not exist in our society" (Walker, *The Guardian*, 04/02/2017).

6 The use of the singular and hyphens here is more than a syntax resource. I intend to reflect with them a true rigid anchorage of the three categories.

BIBLIOGRAPHY

Abi-Rached, J. & Rose, N. (2010). The bird of the neuromolecular gaze. *History of the Human Sciences*, 23(1), 11–36.

American Psychiatric Association (APA) (1980). *Diagnostic and statistical manual of mental disorders* (3rd ed.). Washington, DC: American Psychiatric Association.

American Psychiatric Association (APA) (1994). *Diagnostic and statistical manual of mental disorders* (4th ed.). Washington, DC: American Psychiatric Association.

American Psychiatric Association (APA) (2002). *Diagnostic and statistical manual of mental disorders* (4th ed., Text Revision). Washington, DC: American Psychiatric Association.

American Psychiatric Association (APA) (2013). *Diagnostic and statistical manual of mental disorders* (5th ed.). Washington, DC: American Psychiatric Association.

Austin, J. (1962). *How to do things with words*. Oxford: Oxford University Press.

Bakhtin, M. (1986). *Speech genres and other late essays*. Austin: University of Texas Press.

Baldiz, M. (2010). El psicoanálisis contemporáneo frente a las transexualidades. In M. Missé & G. Coll-Planas (Eds.), *El género desordenado. Críticas en torno a la patologización de la transexualidad* (pp. 141–155). Madrid: Egales.

Balza, I. (2009). Bioética de los cuerpos sexuados: transexualidad, intersexualidad y transgenerismo. *ISEGORÍA. Revista de Filosofía Moral y Política*, 40, 245–258. Retrieved from www.acuedi.org/ddata/11259.pdf

Bauman, Z. (1992). *Mortality, immortality and other life strategies*. Stanford, CA: Stanford University Press.

Bean, R. (1906). Some racial peculiarities of the Negro brain. *American Journal of Anatomy*, 5, 353–415.

Berguero, T. & Cano, G. (2006). Capítulo 7: El proceso diagnóstico. In E. Gómez & I. Esteva de Antonio (Eds.), *Ser transexual. Dirigido al paciente, a su familia, y al entorno sanitario, jurídico y social* (pp. 125–132). Barcelona: Glosa.

Berlant, L. & Warner, M. (1998). Sex in public. *Critical Inquiry*, 24(2), 547–566. Retrieved from https://doi.org/10.1086/448884

Bersani, L. (2010). *Is the rectum a grave? And other essays*. Chicago: University of Chicago Press.

Billings, D. & Urban, T. (1982). The socio-medical construction of transsexualism: An interpretation and critique. *Social Problems*, 29(3), 266–282.

Bonet, J. (2007). Problematizar las políticas sociales frente a la(s) violencia(s) de género. In B. Biglia & C. San Martín (Coords.), *Estado de Wonderbra: Entretejiendo narraciones feministas sobre las violencias de género* (pp. 35–48). Barcelona: Virus.

Borillo, D. (2001). *Homofobia*. Barcelona: Bellaterra.

Bornstein, K. (1994). *Gender outlaw: On men, women and the rest of us*. New York: Routledge.

Bourdieu, P. (1990). *In other words: Essays towards a reflexive sociology*. Stanford, CA: Stanford University Press.

Bourdieu, P. (1998/2001). *Masculine domination*. Stanford, CA: Stanford University Press.

Bourdieu, P., Chamboredon, J.C. & Passeron, J.C. (1973/2002). *El Oficio de Sociólogo. Presupuestos epistemológicos*. Buenos Aires: Siglo Veintiuno editores.

Braidotti, R. (2001). Becoming-woman: Rethinking the positivity of difference. In E. Bronfen & M. Kavka (Eds.), *Feminist consequences: Theory for the new century* (pp. 381–413). New York: Columbia University Press.

Burman, E. (1992). Feminism and discourse in developmental psychology: Power, subjectivity and interpretation. *Feminism & Psychology*, 2(1), 45–60.

Burman, E. (1996). The crisis in modern social psychology and how to find it. *South African Journal of Psychology*, 26(3), 135–142.

Burman, E. (2003). From difference to intersectionality: Challenges and resources. *European Journal of Psychotherapy & Counselling*, 6(4), 293–308.

Butler, J. (1988). Performative acts and gender constitution: An essay in phenomenology and feminist theory. *Theatre Journal*, 40(4), 519–531.

Butler, J. (1990/1999). *Gender trouble: Feminism and the subversion of identity*. New York: Routledge.

Butler, J. (1992). Sexual inversions. In D. C. Stanton (Ed.), *Discourses of sexuality. From Aristotle to AIDS* (pp. 344–361). Ann Arbor: University of Michigan Press.

Butler, J. (1993a). *Bodies that matter. On the discursive limits of "sex"*. New York: Routledge.

Butler, J. (1993b). Critically queer. *GLQ: A Journal of Lesbian and Gay Studies*, 1(1), 17–32.

Butler, J. (1997). *Excitable speech: A politics of the performative*. New York: Routledge.

Butler, J. (2004). *Undoing gender*. New York: Routledge.

Butler, J. (2009a). *Frames of war. When is life grievable?* London: Verso.

Butler, J. (2009b). Performativity, precarity and sexual politics. *Revista de Antropología Iberoamericana*, 4(3), i–xiii.

Butler, J. (2010). Prólogo. Transexualidad, Transformaciones. In M. Missé & G. Coll-Planas (Eds.), *El género desordenado. Críticas en torno a la patologización de la transexualidad* (pp. 9–13). Madrid: Egales.

Caballero, J.P., Lobato, J., Galiano, J., Santana, M. J., Seguera, A.M., Tamayo, A., . . . & Pelluch, A. (2007). Manejo de las complicaciones de la cirugía de reasignación de sexo de mujer a varón. Presentación de 3 casos. *Revista Internacional de Andrología*, 5(4), 398–402.

Cabruja, T. (1996). Posmodernismo y Subjetividad: Construcciones discursivas y relaciones de poder. In A. Gordo & J.L. Linaza (Comps.), *Psicología, Discurso y Poder (PDP): Metodologías cualitativas, perspectivas críticas* (pp. 373–389). Madrid: Visor.

Cabruja, T. (1998). Psicología social crítica y posmodernidad. Implicaciones para las identidades construidas bajo la racionalidad moderna. *Revista Anthropos*, 177, 49–59.

Cabruja, T. (2005). Psicología, racionalidad moderna y producción de la diferencia normal-patológico. In T. Cabruja (Ed.), *Psicología: perspectivas deconstruccionistas. Subjetividad, psicopatología y ciberpsicología* (pp. 115–166). Barcelona: UOC.

Cabruja, T. (2007). Lokas lokuras okupadas. Violencias de la psicología a las mujeres: psicologización, psicopatologización y silenciamiento. In B. Biglia & C. San Martin (Coords.), *Estado de Wonderbra. Entretejiendo narraciones feministas sobre las violencias de género* (pp. 155–170). Barcelona: Virus.

Cabruja, T. (2013). Avenços i reptes actuals de la recerca interdisciplinar sobre des(psico) patologització: tan lluny, tan a prop. *Quaderns de Psicología*, 15(1), 7–20. Retrieved from www.quadernsdepsicologia.cat/article/view/1170

Cabruja, T., Íñiguez, L. & Vázquez, F. (2000). Cómo construimos el mundo: relativismo, espacios de relación y narratividad. *Anàlisi: quaderns de comunicació i cultura*, 25, 61–94. Retrieved from www.raco.cat/index.php/Analisi/article/view/15050

Cabruja, T. & Vázquez, F. (1995). Retórica de la objetividad. *Revista de Psicología Social Aplicada*, 5(1/2), 113–126.

Colás, X. (04/18/2017). Chechenia, el Guantánamo ruso de los gays. *El Mundo*. Retrieved from www.elmundo.es/internacional/2017/04/18/58f513c8e2704e74308b464a.html

Colás, X. (06/30/2013). Putin firma la ley que castiga la propaganda homosexual en Rusia. *El Mundo*. Retrieved from www.elmundo.es/elmundo/2013/06/30/internacional/1372592785.html

Colizzi, M., Costa, R. & Todarello, O. (2014). Transsexual patients' psychiatric comorbidity and positive effect of cross-sex hormonal treatment on mental health: results from a longitudinal study. *Psychoneuroendocrinology*, 39, 65–73.

Coll-Planas, G. (2010a). *La voluntad y el deseo: la construcción social del género y la sexualidad: el caso de lesbianas, gays y trans*. Barcelona: Egales.

Coll-Planas, G. (2010b). La policía del género. In M. Missé & G. Coll-Planas (Eds.), *El género desordenado. Críticas en torno a la patologización de la transexualidad* (pp. 55–66). Madrid: Egales.

Coll-Planas, G., Alfama, E. & Cruells, M. (2013). Se_nos gener@ mujeres. La construcción discursiva del pecho femenino en el ámbito médico. *Athenea Digital*, 13(3), 121–135.

Colombia Diversa (2015). *Cuerpos excluidos, Rostros de impunidad: informe de violencia hacia personas LGBT en Colombia*. Retrieved from http://colombiadiversa.org/

colombiadiversa2016/wp-content/uploads/2016/11/Informe-Violencia-LGBT-Colombia-DDHH-2015.pdf

Connell, R. (2010). Two cans of paint: A transsexual life story, with reflections on gender change and history. *Sexualities*, 13(3), 3–19.

Davies, B. & Harré, R. (1990). Positioning: The discursive production of selves. *Journal for the Theory of Social Behavior*, 20(1), 43–63.

De Cuypere, G., T'Sjoen, G., Beerten, R., Selvaggi, G., De Sutter, P., Hoebeke, P., . . . & Rubens, R. (2005). Sexual and physical health after sex reassignment surgery. *Archives of Sexual Behavior*, 34(6), 679–690.

De Lauretis, T. (1987). *Technologies of gender: Essays on theory, film, and fiction*. Bloomington: Indiana University Press.

De Vos, J. (2013). The subject of the neuropsy-sciences stripped bare by her bachelors, even. *Quaderns de Psicología*, 15(1), 95–106. Retrieved from http://ddd.uab.cat/pub/quapsi/quapsi_a2013v15n1/quapsi_a2013v15n1p95.pdf

Derrida, J. (2001). *Papier machine: le ruban de machine à écrire et autres réponses*. Paris: Galilée.

Diamond, M. & Sigmundson, H. (1997). Sex reassignment at birth. A long-term review and clinical implications. *Archives of Pediatrics & Adolescent Medicine*, 151(3), 298–304.

Dreger, A. (1998). Ambiguous sex or ambivalent medicine? Ethical issues in the treatment of intersexuality. *Hasting Center Report*, 28(3), 24–35.

Edelman, L. (2004). *No future. Queer theory and the death drive*. Durham, NC: Duke University Press.

Eribon, D. (1999/2004). *Insult and the making of the gay self*. Durham, NC: Duke University Press.

Eribon, D. (2000). *Identidades: reflexiones sobre la cuestión gay*. Barcelona: Bellaterra.

Espejo, B. (2009). *Manifiesto puta*. Barcelona: Bellaterra.

European Network of Legal Experts in the Non-discrimination Field (2012). *Trans and intersex people: Discrimination on the grounds of sex, gender identity and gender expression*. Retrieved from http://ec.europa.eu/justice/discrimination/files/trans_and_intersex_people_web3_en.pdf

Fairclough, N. (1989/2001). *Language and power*. Harlow: Pearson Education.

Fairclough, N. (1992/2000). *Discourse and social change*. Cambridge: Polity Press.

Fausto-Sterling, A. (1993). The five sexes: Why male and female are not enough. *Sciences* (May/April), 20–24.

Fausto-Sterling, A. (2000). *Sexing the body: Gender politics and the construction of sexuality*. New York: Basic Books.

Fernández, A.M. (1993/2010). *La mujer de la ilusión*. Buenos Aires: Paidós.

Fernández, S. (2010). Derechos sanitarios desde el reconocimiento de la diversidad. Alternativas a la violencia de la psiquiatrización de las identidades trans. In M. Missé & G. Coll-Planas (Eds.), *El género desordenado. Críticas en torno a la patologización de la transexualidad* (pp. 177–194). Madrid: Egales.

Fisher, A. (2003). Devenires, cuerpos sin órganos, lógica difusa e intersexuales. In D. Maffia (Comp.), *Sexualidades migrantes: Género y transgénero* (pp. 9–30). Buenos Aires: Feminaria.

Foucault, M. (1961/2006). *History of madness.* London: Routledge.

Foucault, M. (1963/2003). *The birth of the clinic: An archaeology of medical perception.* London: Routledge.

Foucault, M. (1969/1972). *The archaeology of knowledge and the discourse on language.* New York: Pantheon Books.

Foucault, M. (1975/1995). *Discipline and punish. The birth of the prison.* New York: Vintage Books.

Foucault, M. (1976/1978). *The history of sexuality. Volume I: An introduction.* New York: Pantheon Books.

Foucault, M. (1976/2003). *Society must be defended. Lectures at the Collège de France, 1975–76.* New York: PICADOR.

Foucault, M. (1977/1994). *Dits et Écrits III.* Paris: Gallimard.

Foucault, M. (1979/1994). *Dits et Écrits IV.* Paris: Gallimard.

Foucault, M. (1980). *Herculine Barbin: Being the recently discovered memoirs of a nineteenth-century French hermaphrodite.* New York: Pantheon Books.

Foucault, M. (1999/2003). *Abnormal. Lectures at the Collége de France 1974–1975.* London: Verso.

Frignet, H. (2000/2003). *El transexualismo.* Buenos Aires: Nueva Visión.

Fuss, D. (Ed.). (1991). *Inside/out. Lesbian theories, gay theories.* New York: Routledge.

Gamson, J. (1995). Must identity movements self-destruct? A queer dilemma. *Social Problems*, 42(3), 390–407.

Garaizabal, C. (1998). La transgresión del género: transexualidades, un reto apasionante. In J.A. Nieto (Ed.), *Transexualidad, transgenerismo y cultura: antropología, identidad y género* (pp. 39–62). Madrid: Talasa.

Garaizabal, C. (2010). Transexualidades, identidades y feminismos. In M. Missé & G. Coll-Planas (Eds.), *El género desordenado. Críticas en torno a la patologización de la transexualidad* (pp. 125–140). Madrid: Egales.

García, S. & Romero, C. (2012). Los desplazamientos políticos de las categorías médicas: actores, discursos y relaciones en la controversia "alteraciones del desarrollo sexual" versus "intersexualidad". In E. Pérez & R. Ibáñez (Eds.), *Cuerpos y Diferencias* (pp. 213–240). Madrid: Plaza y Valdés Editores.

Gold, I. & Stoljar, D. (1999). A neuron doctrine in the philosophy of neuroscience. *Behavioral and Brain Sciences*, 22, 809–869.

Gómez, E., Esteva de Antonio, I. & Fernández-Tresguerres, J. (2006). Causas o fundamentos fisiológicos. In E. Gómez & I. Esteva de Antonio (Eds.), *Ser transexual. Dirigido al paciente, a su familia, y al entorno sanitario, jurídico y social* (pp. 113–124). Barcelona: Glosa.

Gómez, E., Vidal-Hagemeijer, A. & Salamero-Baró, M. (2008). MMPI-2 characteristics of transsexuals requesting sex reassignment: Comparison of patients in prehormonal and presurgical phases. *Journal of Personality Assessment*, 90(4), 1–7.

Gómez-Gil, E., Zubiaurre-Elorza, L., Esteva, I., Guillamon, A., Godás, T., Cruz Almaraz, M., . . . & Salamero, M. (2012). Hormone-treated transsexuals report less social distress, anxiety and depression. *Psychoneuroendocrinology*, 37(5), 662–670.

González, M. (2005). Valores de una ciencia impura. *ARBOR: Ciencia, pensamiento y cultura*, 181(716), 501–514.

Gordo, A. (1995). Un análisis cualitativo y discursivo de los programas clínicos de cambio de sexo: Transexualismo, "travestíes" y otros objetos límite. *Revista de Psicología Social Aplicada*, 5(1/2), 127–145.

Gordo, A. & Parker, I. (Eds.). (1999). *Cyberpsychology*. New York: Routledge.

Grant, L. (1994). *Sexing the millennium*. New York: Grove Press.

Grice, P. (1975). Logic and conversation. In P. Cole & J. Morgan (Eds.), *Syntax and semantics 3: Speech acts* (pp. 41–58). New York: Academic Press.

Haraway, D. (1991). *Simians, cyborgs and women: The reinvention of nature*. New York: Routledge.

Haraway, D. (1997). *Modest_Witness@Second_Millennium. FemaleMan©_Meets_Onco-Mouse™: Feminism and Technoscience*. New York: Routledge.

Hausman, B. (1992). Demanding subjectivity: Transsexualism, medicine, and the technologies of gender. *Journal of the History of Sexuality*, 3(2), 270–302.

Hausman, B. (1995). *Changing sex. Transsexualism, technology, and the idea of gender*. Durham, NC: Duke University Press.

Hirshbein, L. (2010). Sex and gender in psychiatry: A view from history. *Journal of Medical Humanities*, 31(2), 155–170. Retrieved from https://doi.org/10.1007/s10912-010-9105-5

Hook, D. & Parker, I. (2002). Deconstruction, psychopathology and dialectics. *South African Journal of Psychology*, 32(2), 49–54.

Human Rights Watch (06/11/2013). *Russia: Drop homophobic law*. Retrieved from www.hrw.org/news/2013/06/10/russia-drop-homophobic-law

Ibáñez, J. (1979/2003). *Más allá de la sociología. El grupo de discusión: Técnica y crítica*. Madrid: Siglo XXI.

Ibáñez, T. (1996). Construccionismo y Psicología. In A. Gordo & J.L. Linaza (Comps.), *Psicología, Discurso y Poder (PDP): Metodologías cualitativas, perspectivas críticas* (pp. 325–338). Madrid: Visor.

Jordan, N. (Director) (1992). *The crying game*. Ireland and England: Miramax.

Kessler, S. (1998). The medical construction of gender. Case management of intersexual infants. In P. Hopkins (Ed.), *Sex/machine. Readings in culture, gender, and technology*. Bloomington: Indiana University Press.

Kessler, S. (1998/2002). *Lessons from the intersexed*. New Brunswick, NJ: Rutgers University Press.

Kitzinger, C. (1987/1989). *The social construction of lesbianism*. London: Sage.

Kitzinger, C. (1999). Intersexuality: Deconstructing the sex/gender binary. *Feminism & Psychology*, 9(4), 493–498. Retrieved from https://doi.org/10.1177/0959353599009004016

Kristeva, J. (1982). *Powers of horror. An essay on abjection*. New York: Columbia University Press.

Lacan, J. (1936/2001). The mirror stage as formative of the function of the I as revealed in psychoanalitic experience. In *Écrits: A selection* (pp. 1–7). London: Routledge.

Laqueur, T. (1990/2003). *Making sex: Body and gender from the Greeks to Freud*. Cambridge, MA: Harvard University Press.

Llamas, R. (1998). *Teoría torcida: prejuicios y discursos en torno a "la homosexualidad"*. Madrid: Siglo XXI.

Lombardo, M., Ashwin, E., Auyeung, B. & Chakraba, B. (2012). Fetal programming effects of testosterone on the reward system and behavioral approach tendencies in humans. *Biological Psychiatry*, 72(10), 839–847.

Longino, H. (1990). *Science as social knowledge*. Princeton, NJ: Princeton University Press.

Lozano, E. (2009). *Transexuales y cyborgs: obstáculos en el pensamiento de Le Breton*. Paper presented in the V Jornada de Jóvenes Investigadores, Universidad de Buenos Aires. Retrieved from http://webiigg.sociales.uba.ar/iigg/jovenes_investigadores/5jornadasjovenes/EJE7/Lozano_Transexuales_y_cyborgs.pdf

Maffia, D. & Cabral, M. (2003). Los sexos ¿son o se hacen? In D. Maffia (Comp.), *Sexualidades migrantes: Género y transgénero* (pp. 86–96). Buenos Aires: Feminaria.

Martínez, M. (2005). Mi cuerpo no es mío. Transexualidad masculina y presiones sociales de sexo. In Grupo de Trabajo Queer (Eds.), *El eje del mal es heterosexual. Figuraciones, movimientos y prácticas feministas queer* (pp. 113–129). Madrid: Traficantes de sueños.

Martínez-Gúzman, A. & Iñiguez-Rueda, L. (2010). La fabricación del Trastorno de Identidad Sexual: estrategias discursivas en la patologización de la transexualidad. *Discurso y Sociedad*, 4(1), 30–51. Retrieved from www.dissoc.org/ediciones/v04n01/DS4%281%29Martinez&Iniguez.pdf

Mercader (1994/1997). *La ilusión transexual*. Buenos Aires: Nueva Visión.

Mira, A. (2004). *De Sodoma a Chueca. Una historia cultural de la homosexualidad en España del Siglo XX*. Madrid: Egales.

Missé, M. (2010). Epílogo. In M. Missé & G. Coll-Planas (Eds.), *El género desordenado. Críticas en torno a la patologización de la transexualidad* (pp. 265–275). Madrid: Egales.

Missé, M. & Coll-Planas, G. (Eds.). (2010). *El género desordenado. Críticas en torno a la patologización de la transexualidad*. Barcelona: Egales.

Molina, C. (2003). Género y poder desde sus metáforas. Apuntes para una topografía del patriarcado. In S. Tubert (Ed.), *Del sexo al Género: los equívocos de un concepto* (pp. 123–159). Madrid: Cátedra.

Monstrey, S. & Hoebeke, P. (2003). Cirugía de reasignación de sexo en transexuales de hombre a mujer. In A. Becerra-Fernández (Comp.), *Transexualidad: La búsqueda de una identidad* (pp. 143–152). Madrid: Díaz de Santos.

Namaste, V. (2005). *Sex change, social change: Reflections on identity, institutions, and imperialism*. Toronto: Women's Press.

National Center for Transgender Equality and the National Gay and Lesbian Task Force (2009). *National transgender discrimination survey*. Retrieved from www.thetaskforce.org/static_html/downloads/reports/fact_sheets/transsurvey_prelim_findings.pdf

Nieto, J.A. (2008). *Transexualidad, intersexualidad y dualidad de género*. Barcelona: Bellaterra.

Ortega, E. & Romero, C. (2012). *Prácticas médicas de la diferencia sexual: La regulación de los tránsitos en cuerpos trans*. Paper presented in VII Congreso de la Sociedad de Lógica, Metodología y Filosofía de la Ciencia en España, Santiago de Compostela.

Oudshoorn, N. (1994/2005). *Beyond the natural body: An archeology of sex hormones*. London: Routledge.

Parker, I. (1992). *Discourse dynamics: Critical analysis for social and individual psychology.* London: Routledge.

Parker, I. (1996). Discurso, Cultura y Poder en la vida cotidiana. In A. Gordo & J.L. Linaza (Comps.), *Psicología, Discurso y Poder (PDP): Metodologías cualitativas, perspectivas críticas* (pp. 79–92). Madrid: Visor.

Parker, I. (2007). *Revolution in psychology: Alienation to emancipation.* London: Pluto Press.

Potter, J. (1996). *Representing reality. Discourse, rhetoric and social construction.* London: Sage.

Potter, J. & Mulkay, M. (1982). Making theory useful: Utility accounting in social psychologists' discourse. *Fundamenta Scientiae*, 3, 259–258.

Preciado, B. (2000/2011). *Manifiesto contrasexual.* Barcelona: Anagrama.

Preciado, B. (2003). Multitudes queer: Notes pour une politique des "anormaux". *Revue Multitudes*, 12. Retrieved from www.multitudes.net/Multitudes-queer/

Preciado, B. (2004). *Saberes vampiros.* Retrieved from www.mazmorra.com.ar/foro/temas-generales/teoria-queer-saberes-vampiro-de-beatriz-preciado

Preciado, B. (2005). Devenir bollo-lobo o cómo hacerse un cuerpo queer a partir de El pensamiento heterosexual. In D. Córdoba, J. Sáez & P. Vidarte (Eds.), *Teoría queer: políticas bolleras, maricas, trans, mestizas* (pp. 111–131). Madrid: Egales.

Preciado, B. (2010). *Pornotopía. Arquitectura y sexualidad en "Playboy" durante la Guerra Fría.* Barcelona: Anagrama.

Preciado, P. (2008/2015). *Testo Yonqui.* Barcelona: Espasa Calpe.

Punset, E. (2007). *El cerebro tiene sexo (Capítulo REDES 434).* Retrieved from www.youtube.com/watch?v=U969XkI0Bog

Read, J. (2005). The bio-bio-bio model of madness. *Psychologist*, 18(10), 596–597.

Rich, A. (1980/2003). Compulsory heterosexuality and lesbian existence. *Journal of Women's History*, 15(3), 11–48.

Roberts, D. (1997). *Killing the black body: Race, reproduction and the meaning of liberty.* New York: Vintage Books.

Rose, N. (1985). *The psychological complex: Psychology, politics and society in England, 1869–1939.* London: Routledge and Kegan Paul.

Rose, N. (1989). *Governing the soul: The shaping of the private self.* London: Routledge.

Rose, N. (2007). Terapia y Poder: Techné y Ethos. *Archipiélago. Cuadernos de crítica de la cultura*, 76, 101–124.

Roselló, M. (2013). Entre cuerpos inacabados e identidades imposibles: La (psico) patologización de la transexualidad en el discurso psiquiátrico. *Quaderns de Psicología*, 15(1), 57–67. Retrieved from www.quadernsdepsicologia.cat/article/view/1162/880

Roselló, M. & Cabruja, T. (2012). Bio-Ciencia-Ficción: La biologización de la identidad en los discursos médicos y clínicos de la transexualidad. *Quaderns de Psicología*, 14(2), 111–123. Retrieved from www.quadernsdepsicologia.cat/article/view/1145/867

Rubin, G. (1975). The traffic in women: notes on the "political economy" of sex. In R. Reiter (Ed.), *Toward an anthropology of women* (pp. 157–210). New York: Monthly Review Press.

Rubin, H. (2003). *Self-made men. Identity and embodiment among transsexual men.* Nashville, TN: Vanderbilt University Press.

Sancho, R. (2005). Animació: Adolescència i risc: factors de protecció des de l'animació juvenil. *Revista Animació*, 18. Retrieved from http://www.ivaj.gva.es/documents/164427600/164429809/2005.-+N%C2%BA%2018+Adolesc%C3%A8ncia+i+risc+Factors+de+protecci%C3%B3%20des+de+l%E2%80%99 animaci%C3%B3%20juvenil+%28primer+semestre%29/c03c5aa5-7fa3-4ebe-95e7-62be35c29484

Santander, P. (2011). Por qué y cómo hacer análisis del discurso. *Cinta de Moebio*, 41, 207–224. Retrieved from www.facso.uchile.cl/publicaciones/moebio/41/santander.pdf

Sartre, J.P. (1952/1963). *Saint Genet: Actor and martyr*. New York: Plume.

Searle, J. (1969/2011). *Speech acts: An essay in the philosophy of language*. Cambridge: Cambridge University Press.

Sedgwick, E. (1990). *Epistemology of the closet*. Berkeley: University of California Press.

Soley-Beltrán, P. (2005). In-transit: la transexualidad como migración de género. *Asparkia. Investigación feminista*, 15, 207–232. Retrieved from www.e-revistes.uji. es/index.php/asparkia/article/view/821/733

Soley-Beltrán, P. (2013). ¿Buen sexo o sexo de verdad? Perspectivas sobre la regulación del género. *Quaderns de Psicología*, 15(1), 45–56. Retrieved from www.quaderns depsicologia.cat/article/view/1163

Spectrum Human Rights Alliance (08/07/2013). *Recent neo-Nazi victim dies. Anti-Nazi activist in danger!* Retrieved from https://sites.google.com/a/spectrumhr. org/www/hot-news-1/recentneonazivictimdiesanti-naziactivistsindanger?tmpl=%2Fsystem%2Fapp%2Ftemplates%2Fprint%2F&showPrintDialog=1

Spivak, G. (1999). *A critique of postcolonial reason. Toward a history of the vanishing present*. Cambridge, MA: Harvard University Press.

Stoller, R. (1985). *Presentations of gender*. New Haven, CT: Yale University Press.

Stone, S. (1991). The empire strikes back: A posttransexual manifesto. In J. Epstein & K. Straub (Eds.), *Body guards. The cultural politics of gender ambiguity* (pp. 280–304). New York: Routledge.

Swaab, D. & Hofman, M. (1995). Sexual differentiation of the human hypothalamus in relation to gender and sexual orientation. *Trends Neurosciences*, 18(6), 264–270.

Tamagne, F. (2000/2006). *A history of homosexuality in Europe. Volume I & II: Berlin, London, Paris 1919–1939*. New York: Algora.

Taylor, A. (09/04/2017). Reports of anti-gay purges in Chechnya lead to international outrage. *Washington Post*. Retrieved from www.washingtonpost.com/news/worldviews/wp/2017/04/14/reports-of-anti-gay-purges-in-chechnya-lead-to-international-outrage/?utm_term=.3be6808a5d0c

Toldrà, M. (2000). *Capacidad natural y capacidad matrimonial. La transexualidad*. Barcelona: Cedecs.

Tosh, J. (2011a). "Zuck Off"! A commentary on the protest against Ken Zucker and his "treatment" of childhood gender identity disorder. *Psychology of Women Section Review*, 13(1), 10–16.

Tosh, J. (2011b). Academic debate or transphobic hate? A response to "Zuckergate". *Clinical Psychology Forum*, 221, 51–54.

Tosh, J. (2014). *Perverse psychology: The pathologization of sexual violence and transgenderism*. London: Routledge.

Transgender Europe-TGEU (2016). *Trans rights Europe index 2016*. Retrieved from https://tgeu.org/wp-content/uploads/2016/05/trans-map-B-july2016.pdf

Ussher, J. (1989). *The psychology of the female body*. Florence: Taylor and Francis/Routledge.

Vásquez, A. (2012). Foucault: "Los Anormales", una genealogía de lo monstruoso. Apuntes para una historiografía de la locura. *Nómadas. Critical Journal of Social and Juridical Sciences*, 34(2). Retrieved from http://revistas.ucm.es/index.php/NOMA/article/view/40745/39064

Vázquez, F. & Moreno, A. (1997). *Sexo y razón: una genealogía de la moral sexual en España (siglo XVI–XX)*. Madrid: AKAL.

Walker, S. (04/02/2017). Chechen police "have rounded up more than 100 suspected gay men". *The Guardian*. Retrieved from www.theguardian.com/world/2017/apr/02/chechen-police-rounded-up-100-gay-men-report-russian-newspaper-chechnya

Wierckx, K., Van Caenegem, E., Elaut, E., Dedecker, D., Van de Peer, F., Toye, K., . . . & T'Sjoen, G. (2011). Quality of life and sexual health after sex reassignment surgery in transsexual men. *Journal of Sexual Medicine*, 8(12), 3379–3388.

Wilchins, R. (1997). *Read my lips. Sexual subversion and the end of gender*. Ithaca, NY: Firebrand Books.

Wilkinson, S. & Kitzinger, C. (Eds.) (1994). *Women and health: Feminist perspectives*. London: Taylor & Francis.

Wittig, M. (1992). *The straight mind and other essays*. Boston: Beacon Press.

World Professional Association for Transgender Health, WPATH (2011). *Standards of care for the health of transsexual, transgender, and gender nonconforming people* (7th version). Retrieved from www.wpath.org

INDEX